Library of
Davidson College

A Dante Of Our Time

American University Studies

Series II
Romance Languages and Literature
Vol. 134

PETER LANG
New York • Bern • Frankfurt am Main • Paris

Risa B. Sodi

A Dante Of Our Time

Primo Levi and Auschwitz

PETER LANG
New York • Bern • Frankfurt am Main • Paris

Library of Congress Cataloging-in-Publication Data

Sodi, Risa B.
   A Dante of our time : Primo Levi and Auschwitz / Risa B. Sodi.
      p. cm. — (American university studies. Series II, Romance languages and literature ; vol. 134)
   Includes bibliographical references.
   1. Levi, Primo—Criticism and interpretation. 2. Dante Alighieri, 1265-1321—Influence—Levi. 3. Dante Alighiere, 1265-1321. Inferno. 4. Levi, Primo. Se questo è un uomo. 5. Levi, Primo. Sommersi e i salvati. 6. Justice in literature. I. Title. II. Series.
PQ4872.E8Z88   1990   853'.914—dc20   90-5535
ISBN 0-8204-1219-8   CIP
ISSN 0740-9257

CIP-Titelaufnahme der Deutschen Bibliothek

Sodi, Risa B.:
A Dante of our time : Primo Levi and Auschwitz / Risa B. Sodi. – New York; Bern; Frankfurt am Main; Paris: Lang, 1990.
   (American University Studies: Ser. 2, Romance Languages and Literature; Vol. 134)
   ISBN 0-8204-1219-8

NE: American University Studies / 02

© Peter Lang Publishing, Inc., New York 1990

All rights reserved.
Reprint or reproduction, even partially, in all forms such as microfilm, xerography, microfiche, microcard, offset strictly prohibited.

Printed by Weihert-Druck GmbH, Darmstadt, West Germany

To my mother

ACKNOWLEDGEMENTS

I would like to acknowledge the help and encouragement of Professors Frederick Busi, Thomas Cassirer, Roland Sarti, Jennifer Stone and Sara Sturm Maddox of the University of Massachusetts at Amherst, and Prof. Howard Adelman of Smith College, as well as the generous technical help provided by Margaret Burggren.

My parents and my husband, Stefano, were also unwavering in their support and encouragement.

CONTENTS

Introduction 1

1. *Al di qua del bene e del male*: Justice in Dante's *Inferno* and in Primo Levi's First and Last Books................... 5

2. Neither *in bono* nor *in malo*: The Grey Zone and the Neutral Sinners... 31

3. Obliviscence and Reminiscence: Memory and the Memory of Offense.. 49

Conclusion.. 81

Notes... 91

Bibliography... 103

Index... 109

INTRODUCTION

Why trace Primo Levi's development by comparing and contrasting it to Dante, poet of the inferno, master fantasist, as able with allegory as with truth, devout Christian, defeated potitician? What can the bard of the *trecento* have to say to the memorialist of the Holocaust? Why compare a fictional inferno to a real one?

Even admitting the enormous differences of age, style, and orientation between Levi and Dante, one still cannot overlook the strange kinship that binds these two artists together. Primo Levi's first and last books, *Se questo è un uomo* and *I sommersi e i salvati* and Dante's *Inferno* bear striking affinities. This should not be wholly surprising since Levi received a classical education in Italy at a time when Dante still occupied a central place in secondary schooling.[1]

Nonetheless, Levi draws on Dante in such a knowledgeable and meaningful way as to make their connection more than just circumstantial. Levi quotes Dante repeatedly, from the moving "Canto di Ulisse" chapter in *Se questo è un uomo* to the Dantesque title of *I sommersi e i salvati* (which, incidentally, was the original working title of *Se questo è un uomo*). His conversations were littered with quotations from the *Commedia*; in an interview with me, Levi used Conte Ugolino to help prove his point about the memory of offense and Fra Alberigo illustrated his comments on the Nazis' view of the Jews.[2] Taken together, even these few tidbits point to the formidable intellectual debt that Levi owed Dante. Still, they are but a small part of the heart of the current analysis and only the springboard that occasioned this study of Primo Levi and Dante.

Levi's first and last books reveal a substantial communality of themes and structure vis-à-vis the *Inferno*. The three works are nearly congeneric as they struggle with a definition of justice and ponder the weight of memory on a person's soul. The also posit an analogous moral construct–for Levi, *la zona grigia*, for Dante, the realm of the neutral sinners–where categories of victims and oppressors, sinners and saints blur ever so slightly but decisively.

This study sets out to analyze these three affinities in three separate chapters, and also to explore the often surprising ways in which the three themes are linked. The primarly focus will be Primo Levi–some years after his death, still the most compelling voice in contemporary Italian letters–though this study will also try to illustrate, through ample analysis of the *Inferno*, how Levi's message is often clearest when filtered through Dante.

It is particularly appropriate to this study of Primo Levi and the *Inferno* that Levi, in the very first pages of *Se questo è un uomo* occupies himself with the question of justice, and in the first few pages of *I sommersi e i salvati* turns his attention to memory. These are the two concerns and the two books which will animate much of the discussion of Levi and Dante that will follows. Auschwitz (here taken as the epitome of the Nazi death camps) is the symbol of human injustice, the extreme proof, as Levi says, that "nei contatti umani non c'è legge."[3] The victims of Auschwitz keenly felt the lack of justice, at that time and since. Many works have testified to the six million unanswered voices (Ferruccio De Cori, an Italian Holocaust survivor, calls them "the six million in search of an author") asking such crucial questions as, "Where is justice for Holocaust survivors?" or "How do we interpret the events and the moral legacy of the Holocaust?"

Primo Levi adds his voice to that tumult, yet it is a calm and thoughtful voice, the voice of a man in no hurry to produce an answer and keen on understanding all aspects of the question. In his writings, Levi skillfully blends an author's narrative considerations with measured, almost clinical, analysis. The two books of his under consideration outline moral and human concerns, while their judgments successfully maintain equanimity. When he says, "chi sbaglia paga," he is also referring to himself and other Holocaust victims, and not, as one might expect, to his captors alone.[4] By itself, this harsh sentence at the very beginning of his Auschwitz parable is a clear signpost that the considerations that follow will be difficult, measured, blunt and often painfully true. Levi is a poet of the inferno, but one who keeps his shoulders close to the wall of exactitude.

CHAPTER I

AL DI QUA DEL BENE E DEL MALE: JUSTICE IN DANTE'S *INFERNO* AND IN PRIMO LEVI'S FIRST AND LAST BOOKS

> Alcune psicologi moderni pensano che il senso della giustizia è particolarmente intenso nei perseguitati. Essi rivendicano ardentemente giustizia, e quanto più ne sono privi, tanto più si fanno un'idea elevata, sia del suo valore che dei suoi benefici. Checché ne sia del carattere generale di tale teoria, essa sembra adattarsi perfettamente a Dante e alla sua opera.[1]

This judgment applies just as "perfectly" to Primo Levi as to Dante. Justice is often a central issue in accounts of Auschwitz, just as it is usually invoked whenever there is human suffering. Primo Levi, however, witnessed and survived some of the greatest suffering of our time, and yet he is strangely unforthcoming on the subject of justice. True, his books are peppered with references to justice: as it was perverted in the death camps, as it eludes their survivors, as it was thwarted by many war criminals. And yet, he stops just short of either enunciating a call for justice or of developing his own systematic line of thought. Levi repeatedly refrains from direct judgment of his former oppressors, often absolving those "grey zoners" who were coerced into abetting the Final Solution, and demurs on the issue of justice when analyzing such closely allied elements as the "memory of offense" or "useless" and "useful" violence. At the same time, he frequently repeats the forcefully blunt verdict he implied in his first book-"chi sbaglia paga"-often with redoubled vehemence.[2] Its last formulation came in 1986 when, writing in relation to the Nazi system, he stated baldly, "se l'oppressore soffre, ne è giusto."[3]

In analyzing Primo Levi, how are we to make sense of this man who can both enigmatically renounce judgment and forcefully evoke it? Perhaps a look at what Levi has said and intimated about justice, beginning with his first book and then jumping to his last, in light of several philosophical conceptions of justice, will provide insight into this matter.

Levi's first book begins with a poem, dated January 10, 1946. This poem is an admonition and a cry of pain, and the title of *Se questo è un uomo* comes from one of its verses:

> Voi che vivete sicuri
> Nelle vostre tiepide case,
> Voi che trovate tornando a sera
> Il cibo caldo e visi amici:
>   Considerate se questo è un uomo   5
> Che lavora nel fango
> Che lotta per mezzo pane
> Che muore per un sì o per un no.
> Considerate se questa è una donna,
> Senza capelli e senza nome   10
> Senza più forza di ricordare
> Vuoti gli occhi e freddo il grembo
> Come una rana d'inverno.
> Meditate che questo è stato:
> Vi comando queste parole.   15
> Scolpitele nel vostro cuore

>   Stando in casa andando per via,
>   Coricandovi alzandovi;
>   Ripetetele ai vostri figli.
>   O vi si sfaccia la casa,
>   La malattia vi impedisca,   20
>   I vostri nati torcano il viso da voi.

These few lines allude to a multitude of thematic concerns of Levi's and biographical details about his life. First, written just three months after Levi's circuitous journey back to Italy from Auschwitz (he arrived home in Turin on October 14, 1945), it was one of the first things he wrote after Auschwitz. Second, it is untitled in *Se questo è un uomo*, but when reprinted in *L'osteria di Brema* in 1975, Levi calls it *Shema*, the first word and name of the central section of the Jewish liturgy. Taken from the Bible, this prayer is recited daily and uttered on one's deathbed:

> Hear, O Israel: The Lord Our God, the Lord is One! And these words, which I command thee this day, shall be upon thy heart, and thou shalt teach them diligently unto thy children, and thou shalt talk of them when thou sittest in thy house, and when thou walkest by the way, and when thou liest down, and when thou risest up."[4]

Third, since verses 15 through 20 follow the Hebrew prayer so closely, it affirms the importance of Levi's Jewish roots to his beginnings as an author and the centrality of this heritage and the Sh'ma—Levi's *Shema*—to the book it precedes.

What is significant about this poem, especially for the present study, is its severe and abrupt conclusion (wholly different from the thrust of the traditional prayer): "O vi si sfaccia la casa,/ La malattia vi impedisca,/ I vostri nati torcano il viso da voi."[5] Unlike the verses from the liturgy,

Levi's poem ends with a bleak monition against perverting the traditional order of things envisioned by the Sh'ma. It is an exhortation to present and future generations that ends with the threat of retribution. "Heed my words and my example," Levi seems to say, "or evil will befall you; you will lose your home, your health and the love of your loved ones."

Retribution, in an intuitive sense, is the simplest of the four forms of justice distinguished by contemporary moral and legal philosophers. Morris Ginzberg, in his book *On Justice in Society*, provides an analysis of each of these four types: commutative, distributive, corrective and retributive justice. The first two have to do with the relationships of individuals to each other or of society as a whole to its members; the third type of justice concerns itself with providing redress; and retributive justice pertains to the dispensing of reward or punishment.

While all four types of justice may have various degrees of applicability to Levi and Dante, both writers seem actively concerned with retribution in the works under consideration here. In Dante's case, he employs retribution especially as regards the hereafter; in Levi's case, retribution becomes a factor in analyzing the moral legacy of the Holocaust. The Levi of *Shema* lays down a clear equation in his poem; literally he says: repeat these words to your children lest evil befall you. His general meaning is every bit as ominous: inaction leads to castigation. In this second context, we can say that for Levi, refraining from acting becomes a punishable offense.

There is a noble precendent for Levi's formulation, although it is unlikely it was on his mind as he hastily wrote *Shema* on his return from

Auschwitz. That is Thomas Aquinas' thirteenth-century dictim, *malus est defectus, peccatum est actus*, which Aquinas used to distinguish "simple evil" from "sinful action." This concept will be explored further in Chapter II, especially as it relates to Dante's neutral sinners; for now, suffice it to note the intriguing parallel construction between Aquinas' condemnation of inaction and Levi's formulation of the same equation. It will become especially significant to this study, when we take up the subject of the memory of offense in Chapter III, that the particular inaction Levi roundly denounces is forgetfulness, the lack of memory.

Why does Levi pass over redress? Why does he shun remedial action, compensation, or reparation for punishment? The answer lies in the first chapter of *Se questo è un uomo*. Levi explains that he was captured by the Fascist militia on December 13, 1943. In the naïve belief that the punishment given to an "Italian citizen of the Jewish race" would be, as he later learned, less severe than that given to a partisan, Levi confessed to being a Jew. He was immediately sent to an internment camp in Fossoli (near Modena, in northeastern Italy) and, a few months later, was shipped in a sealed freight car to Poland.[6] What he categorizes as an error of judgment, choosing one identity instead of another, meant eleven months and near death at Auschwitz.

Does Levi evoke the reader's compassion for such an ingenuous and human error? Does he express remorse? The answer is stunning and indicative of the tone of the rest of the book: Levi's reaction is not self-pity but self-reproach:

A quel tempo, non mi era stata ancora insegnata la dottrina che dovevo

> A quel tempo, non mi era stata ancora insegnata la dottrina che dovevo più tardi rapidamente imparare in *Lager*, e secondo il quale il primo ufficio dell'uomo è perseguire i propri scopi con mezzi idonei, e chi sbaglia paga; per cui non posso che considerare conforme a giustizia il successivo svolgersi dei fatti.[7]

Levi judges himself with no excess compassion. His aim is instead to show the reader that all people are subject to certain standards, even when, as in this case, it is the victim (Levi) who must suffer the consequences. Look!, he seems to say, even in critical times, the common laws of human interaction must remain constant.

Much of Levi's work is dedicated to explicating and delineating the boundaries between various fundamental propositions that shape the ontological makeup of a person. Many of these, he writes in *La ricerca delle radici*, take the form of key oppositions inscribed "*ex officio* nel destino di ogni uomo cosciente": truth/error, laughter/tears, wisdom/folly, hope/desperation, victory/defeat.[8] To this list, we must certainly add justice and injustice.[9] However, the important words in this recipe are not the oppositions themselves but the two words "uomo cosciente." We have just told a story about Levi's capture and his subsequent admission to being an Italian Jew. In that circumstance, Levi, as a rational man, was faced with a choice between two uncertain alternatives: admitting his partisan activities or volunteering his religious affiliation.[10] He chose the latter option and far from ruing the consequences, accepts them as just. *Chi sbaglia paga.*

The notion of intent or volition is central to most concepts of justice and is also important in any discussion of punishment. When Levi puts his former oppressors to the intentionality test, he finds they meet all the criteria. He states quite clearly that, in spite of the tremendous pressures exercised on the ordinary citizen by totalitarian regimes, the Nazi oppressors adhered to the mechanics of the Third Reich voluntarily–intentionally.

> La pressione che un moderno Stato totalitario può esercitare sull'individuo è paurosa. Le sue armi sono sostanzialmente tre: la propaganda diretta, o camuffata da educazione, da istruzione, da cultura popolare; lo sbarramento opposto al pluralismo delle informazioni; il terrore. Tuttavia, non è lecito ammettere che questa pressione sia irresistibile, tanto meno nel breve termine dei dodici anni del Terzo Reich: nelle affermazioni e nelle discolpe di uomini dalle gravissime responsabilità...è palese l'esagerazione, ed ancor più la manomissione del ricordo.[11]

Western legal systems generally provide safeguards against punishing behavior excusable for reasons of accident, mistake, provocation, duress or insanity.[12] Yet, none of these excuses apply to Nazi behavior during the Holocaust, according to Levi. The tremendous machinery and logistical finesse required to execute the Final Solution was no accident or mistake. Those who manned the machinery and guarded the *Stück* (or "pieces," as the prisoners were called) in large measure were not there due to duress (as the following passage will make clear); their meticulous cruelty was not externally provoked, but rather internally motivated. Lastly, they were insane only in that their actions were beyond the ken of a moral world, not in that they were unable to anticipate or judge the effect of their actions, Levi explains,

> Ci viene chiesto dai giovani, tanto più spesso e tanto più insistentemente quanto più quel tempo si allontana, chi erano, di che stoffa erano fatti, i nostri "aguzzini." Il termine allude ai nostri ex custodi, alle SS, e a mio parere è improprio: fa pensare a individui distorti, nati male, sadici, affetti da un vizio d'origine. Invece erano fatti della nostra stessa stoffa, erano esseri umani medi, mediamente intelligenti, mediamente malvagi: salvo eccezioni, non erano mostri, avevano il nostro viso, ma erano stati educati male. Erano, in massima parte, gregari e funzionari rozzi e diligenti: alcuni fanaticamente convinti del verbo nazista, molti indifferenti, o paurosi di punizioni, o desiderosi di fare carriera, o troppo obbedienti. Tutti avevano subìto la terrificante diseducazione fornita ed imposta dalla scuola quale era stata voluta da Hitler e dai suoi collaboratori, e completata poi dal *Drill* delle SS. A questa milizia parecchi avevano aderito per il prestigio che conferiva, per la sua onnipotenza, o anche solo per sfuggire a difficoltà famigliari. Alcuni, pochissimi per verità, ebbero ripensamenti, chiesero il trasferimento al fronte, diedero cauti aiuti ai prigionieri, o scelsero il suicidio.[13] Sia ben chiaro che responsabili, in grado maggiore o minore, erano tutti, ma dev'essere altrettanto chiaro che dietro la loro responsabilità sta quella della grande maggioranza dei tedeschi, che hanno accettato all'inizio, per pigrizia mentale, per calcolo miope, per stupidità, per orgoglio nazionale, le "belle parole" del caporale Hitler, lo hanno seguito finché la fortuna e la mancanza di scrupoli lo hanno favorito, sono stati travolti dalla sua rovina, funestati da lutti, miseria e rimorsi, e riabilitati pochi anni dopo per uno spregiudicato gioco politico.[14]

If, as the legal philosopher H. L. A. Hart asserts, one must establish the presence of *mens rea* (or an understanding of the crime) in order to inflict punishment on the perpetrator of the same, then it is evident from this passage that Levi would insist on the *mens rea* of his former tormentors.[15] To emphasize the very voluntariness of Nazi actions, Levi introduces a difficult concept to his last book: the concept of "useful violence." This term may seem provocatory or even offensive, he writes, yet unfortunately, *useful* violence–violence with an aim–exists. He cites several examples: war; political assassination (such as Princip at Sarajevo or Aldo Moro on Via Fani); the murder committed by Raskolnikov in *Crime and Punishment*; or death itself–even natural death, which inevitably overtakes us all and yet is a form of "useful violence."[16]

Levi, nonetheless, uses the term "useful violence" in effect to introduce its opposite, *useless* violence and, in particular, to highlight the pervasive useless violence of the *Lager* system. Levi and I turned to this argument in a 1986 discussion at his home in Turin.

> RS: There was a part of your book that I found very disturbing, and that is the concept of useful and useless violence. Can there ever be such a thing as *useful* violence?
>
> PL: I know this is a difficult argument to explain. I have the impression that there are two different levels of cruelty. For example, in *I sommersi e i salvati*, I've written that Raskolnikov's crime, where he kills the old crone so he won't have to pay his debt, is not a useless crime. He doesn't want suffering or death for the old woman; he wants money and murder is his means. By the same token, Aldo Moro was killed in Italy; the Red Brigades didn't want to kill someone or inflict suffering on him or his family: they had a political plan. Instead, many of the Nazis' actions reflect nothing but the desire to inflict suffering for the purpose of inflicting suffering–and nothing more.
>   I've mentioned one clamorous example, of the ninety-year-olds in the Jewish nursing home in Venice who were loaded onto trains and taken away to the camps. Wouldn't it have been much more logical to kill them on the spot? I don't know if my interpretation of this event is right, but I see it as a scheme to inflict the maximum possible suffering on them–or else pure stupidity. When an order reads *alle*, everyone, then everyone must be deported. The Nazis

took their orders literally and deported everyone.

It's a German characteristic to take orders literally, but as I've said, the Germans weren't made from a different mold than we were. Nothing would have happened to them if they had killed the moribund women on the spot. The guards wouldn't have been punished. But I think they derived a malicious pleasure from deporting them. Since they had been fed an intense propaganda campaign, according to which Jews were nothing more than *Ungezieferen*, harmful animals–harmful insects, really–we were treated like harmful insects, like hateful people. There were many who truly hated us and considered it just to make us suffer. There's an episode in *The Divine Comedy* in which Dante inflicts suffering on one of the damned (I believe it's Bocca degli Abbati).[17] He lies in a gelid lake, his eyes frozen over with ice so he can't even weep. This damned soul begs Dante, "I'll tell you my story if only you'll remove the ice from my eyes." Dante has him tell his story and then says,

> I oped them not.
> Rudeness was courtesy to such as he.[18]

In other words, it was Dante's duty to be cruel to him. I think something similar happened in Germany. The feeling that Dante, a fervent Catholic, felt toward the damned, who have lost their rights and who must be forced to suffer, was perhaps the Nazis' position with regard to the Jews: they felt they must be forced to endure the maximum possible suffering.[19]

In *I sommersi e i salvati*, Levi calls this attitude *Schadenfreude*, "la gioia per il danno del prossimo, né tanto meno la gioia del far deliberatemente soffrire."[20]

Levi's reference to Dante is just one of many he made that day when speaking about the idea of justice; it stands alongside similar, numerous references he made to *il sommo poeta*, and especially to the *Inferno*, in nearly all of his books. Just how accurate is Levi's assessment of Dante's idea of justice, and what can the latter tell us that will help illuminate Levi's thoughts on this basic moral quandary?

The most obvious and fundamental difference between Levi and Dante via-à-vis justice is their orientation. To paraphrase a comment made about Elie Weisel and Levi, Dante looks toward with God while Levi interrogates man.[21] Dante in the *Ninth Epistle* characterizes himself as "a man preaching justice."[22] Many of his works, in fact, deal with it in detail (though not the kind of justice that concerns us here). His political treatise, *De Monarchia*, concerns itself heavily with civic and state justice. Dante also planned to include a treatise on temporal justice and ethics in the unfinished *Convivio*.

In the *Commedia*, on the other hand, Dante passes through the inferno in order to see divine justice in its dealings with evil; God's justice is its theme. The famous inscription on the portal of Dis reminds those who pass through it (and all those who read about it) that "Giustizia mosse il mio alto fattore"; through his comments and allegories, Dante demonstrates that in the inferno his attention is focused on the rule of God.[23]

Phillipe Delhaye, a Dante specialist, has written in his essay on justice in the *Enciclopedia dantesca* that, for Dante, justice is "viva, sempiterna e rigida."[24] His perspective is theocratic and theocentric. "Tra tutti gli attributi di Dio, Dante considera con fervore tutto speciale la giustizia vendicativa. Dio, per lui, è soprattutto la potenza sovrana che punisce i malvagi."[25] God the Avenger shows up throughout the *Inferno*, in Cantos VII, XII, XXIX and others:

> Così scendemmo nella quarta lacca,
>   pigliando più de la dolente ripa
>   che 'l mal de l'universo tutto insacca. Ahi
> giustizia di Dio! tante chi stipa
>   nove travaglie e pene quant'io viddi?
> (*Inferno* VII, 16-20)

> La divina giustizia di qua punge
>   quell'Attila che fu flagello in terra
>   e Pirro e Sesto;
> (*Inferno* XII 133-35)

> Noi discendemmo in su l'ultima riva
>   del lungo scoglio, pur da man sinistra,
>   e allor fu la mia vista più viva
> giù ver' lo fondo, la 've la ministra
>   de l'alto sire, infallabil giustizia,
>   punisce i falsador che qui registra.
> (*Inferno* XXIX 52-57)

Delhaye points out that this vision of God was much in line with contemporary preaching, as illustrated, for example, by the late thirteenth-century/early fourteenth-century Baptistry mosaics in Florence. These mosaics incorporate Old Testament themes (like Creation) and figures (such as Joseph) with the more customary gospel elements of the story of Jesus and John the Baptist. According to traditional Christian theology, the Old Testament featured a jealous, wrathful, severe and rancorous God, while the New Testament concerned itself more with pardon and grace. However, as Delhaye points out, the Middle Ages gradually turned from the New Testament to the Old Testament, often mixing the two, and Dante's view of justice reflects this: the God of the *Inferno* punishes the sinners and those who have harmed others with no hope for pardon (nor, as we will see later, no appeal for it from the sinners). God's divine justice, as Dante portrays it, punishes, crams, goads, spurs and is, above all, infallible. In Dante's world, the sinful are punished and the just exempted from punishment.

Dante reflects the Aristotelian view (passed on by Aquinas) that moral virtue is a habit of choice when he says "E nascono tutte [queste virtù] da uno principio, cioè, dall'abito della nostra buona elezione."[26] This *habitus* of sin is responsible for Dante's condemning Ulysses—for many, a great and noble figure—to horrible torment in the eight bolgia. *Habitus* speaks directly to the notion of volition—similar to the idea of voluntariness discussed above in reference to Levi. The importance of volition is shown by the fact that the incontinent sinners (gluttons, heretics, the lascivious, the avaricious, the prodigal, and the wrathful) are housed in higher circles than the dispassionate sinners (the violent and the fraudulent), who are housed in the lowest three circles of hell.[27] The notion of volition is also reflected by the sinners themselves in Canto III who, far from fleeing punishment in hell, are instead anxious to pass through its gates:

> "Figiuol mio," disse l'maestro cortese
> "quelli che muoion nell'ira di Dio
> tutti convegnon qui d'ogne paese;
> e pronti sono a trapassar lo rio,
> ché la divina giustizia li sprona,
> sì che la tema si volve in disio.
> (*Inferno* III 121-26)

Man seeks justice, Dante seems to imply, even when it is in the guise of punishment.

How different this is from the "sinners"–the Nazi war criminals–that Primo Levi writes about in *I sommersi e i salvati*. Instead of seeking justice or claiming their right to be punished, as do the souls in the *Inferno*, they prevaricate, re-elaborate, and tamper with their past all the better to sidestep justice and dodge punishment: "Anche loro, così forti di fronte al dolore altrui, quando il destino li ha messi davanti ai giudici, davanti alla morte che hanno meritato, si sono costruiti un passato di comodo ed hanno finito per credervi."[28] Our civic justice does not have the powers of omniscience with which Dante cloaked himself in the *Inferno*, powers which allowed him to unmask and condemn notables of his time and earlier, and to send such persons as Popes Nicholas and Boniface to the inferno. The contemporary Western system of justice today has no such penetrating vision. It is humanly flawed and subject to varying interpretations and constraints.

Unlike the divine justice Dante preaches, the temporal justice Levi invokes does not have and, perhaps, in Levi's view, does not need infallibility. Levi, in his musings on justice, virtually excludes the rule of God from the rule of man. His appeal is to our sense of fairness as well as to a higher moral order. On these grounds, we can contrast Dante and Levi since Dante would bypass human law for divine law, and Levi, a nonbeliever, would eschew divine law for human law. Levi puts his faith in the court system. His is an institutionalized vision of justice. Accordingly, Levi exposes and condemns institutionalized systems of iniquity, such as the *Lager* system, which controvert basic moral behavior. He gives one example of such topsy-turvy "justice" in *Se questo è un uomo*, in a chapter whose title has also become the title of this chapter: *Al di qua del bene e del male*.

> Il furto in Buna, punito dalla Direzione civile, è autorizzato e incoraggiato dalle SS; il furto in campo, represso severamente dalle SS, è considerato dai civili una normale operazione di scambio; il furto fra *Häftlinge* [prisoners] viene generalmente punito, ma la punizione colpisce con uguale gravità il ladro e il derubato. Vorremmo ora invitare il lettore a riflettere, che cosa potessero significare in *Lager* le nostre parole "bene" e "male", "giusto" e "ingiusto"; giudichi ognuno in base al quadro che abbiamo delineato e agli esempi sopra esposti, quanto del nostro comune mondo morale potesse sussistere al di qua del filo spinato.[29]

Towards the end of *I sommersi e i salvati*, Levi recounts an episode he also included in *Se questo è un uomo*: the story of Elias the dwarf. After being goaded by Elias (a man possessed of neither self-control nor a conscience; the only man, Levi says, who actually enjoyed life in the camp), the two men got into a fistfight. Levi was no match for his tenacious and muscular adversary and Elias quickly pinned him down by the throat, only to let him go without a word at the first signs of approaching unconsciousness.

> Dopo questa conferma [of the results of taking the law into his own hands], preferisco, nei limiti del possibile, delegare punizioni, vendette e ritorsioni alle leggi del mio paese. È una scelta obbligata: so quanto i meccanismi relativi funzionino male, ma io sono quale sono stato costruito dal mio passato, e non mi è più possibile cambiarmi."[30]

If Levi prefers the criminal justice system; if, however, as he admits above, "the mechanisms [of justice] function poorly"; and if, as he argued earlier, many war criminals were quickly rehabilitated due to "ruthless political maneuvering," we must then consider the relative constancy or arbitrariness inherent in human justice in general, and in retribution in particular. The political theorist Milton Kaplan holds that human nature is "dispositional" since "it responds differently in different settings."[31] We might then ask, is human justice also dispositional? Does it, too, change according to the setting and the circumstance? If so, does the inherent nature of human justice then posit the need for a higher, non-arbitrary order of justice?

Dante would certainly concur with the latter statement. His *Inferno*, as we have seen, is based on a divine order of justice. Levi's position is more problematic. His concept of justice is highly institutionalized (and principally enacted through the courts of law). Recent statements of his show that since he himself felt incapable of judging his fellow man, he would leave that task to "judges or rabbis":

> I don't have the authority to bestow forgiveness. If I were a rabbi, maybe I would; if I were a judge, perhaps. I believe that if someone has commited a crime, he has to pay. It's not up to me to say, "I exempt you from punishment." The authority does not rest with me.[32]

When Levi turns to judges or rabbis to pass judgment and bestow forgiveness (though, in Judaism, rabbis do not grant forgiveness), his decision on the one hand is grounded in the rule of law and in accepted moral standards, while on the other, it is based on an intuitive appraisal of the perpetrator's moral condition, such as only a religious can make. A rabbi's forgiveness would be grounded in a higher order than a judge's. When Levi turns to rabbis, is he implicitly acknowledging a human link to divine justice? A statement from *I sommersi e i salvati* seems to point in this direction: "La condizione di offeso [prisoner] non esclude la colpa, e spesso questa è obbiettivamente grave, ma non conosco tribunale umano a cui delegarne la misura."[33] If human courts of law are inadequate, as this statement suggests, then the alternative would have to be some sort of divine tribunal. Therein lies the ambiguity of Levi's position on justice: he forcefully argues for earthly justice yet at the same time obliquely refers—or defers—to divine judgment.

Retribution, a category of justice that is most sympathetic to the philosophical aims of Dante and Levi, is the view that "punishment, by definition, can only be inflicted on the guilty."[34] So it is in the *Inferno*; so it is not in the post-Holocaust world.[35] James Sterba points out in *The Demands of Justice* that retributivism "does not provide a moral justification of the infliction of punishment but an elucidation of the word."[36] Many modern legal theorists shy away from the application of retribution in favor of relativism (according to which, "the concepts of good and just are determined by continual interaction between man and society and the environment,") or utilitarianism (which holds that "punishment should be applied only insofar as it will maximize deterrance").[37]

Both views see retribution as justice for revenge, or as institutionalized vengefulness. Dante and Levi unwittingly counter this accusation with remarkably similar statements. Dante writes in the *Commedia* (speaking about Jason), "tal colpa a tal martirio lui condanna."[38] In other words, his punishment is not exacted out of vengefulness, nor does it exceed his crime; instead, it was provoked by the sinner himself and is the fitting punishment for his offense. Levi says in an abovementioned passage, "...If they committed a crime, then they have to pay because justice doesn't exist if there's no payment."[39] Levi would have little trouble with the rhetorical question posed by Morris Ginsberg in *On Justice in Society*, "Is a combination of wrong-doing and pain inflicted as punishment a lesser evil than wrong-doing unpunished?"[40] He would undoubtedly answer, yes indeed. Thus, it is also appropriate that, when Levi refers to the *Commedia* in his works, it is exclusively to the Dantesque (retributive) justice of the *Inferno* and not to the ethereal, absolutionary justice of *Purgatory* or *Paradise*. It is quite beyond both Dante's intentions in the *Inferno* and Primo Levi's in his various writings to free the subjects of their discourse from punishment or to remit them from penalty.

Nonetheless, retributive justice often becomes mired in the difficulty of apportioning punishment to guilt. Perhaps that explains why Dante's punishments meted out in the *Inferno* are not "apportioned" at all but are instead poetically applied through the *contrapasso* (a mechanism whereby the offense is mirrored in the punishment). As Alan Gilbert, a Dante scholar, points out, the *Commedia* "cannot be morally or even aesthetically acceptable unless the punishments and rewards of which it treats are accepted as justly assigned."[41] In the *Inferno*, crime and sin meet their punishment in the form of the *contrapasso*. Dante organized his system of justice both doctrinally and topographically, so that like sins were classified together and each successive circle housed a graver sin. As he descended into the great pit and met each group of sinners, Dante also observed their *contrapasso*, the fitting punishment for each sinner's crime.

The scriptural basis for the *contrapasso* was the Mosaic *lex talionis*, or law of retribution. Enunciated in Exodus 21:22-25 ("...if any harm follows, then you shall give life for life, eye for eye, tooth for tooth, hand for hand, foot for foot, burn for burn, wound for wound, stripe for stripe"), it is repeated in similar form in Leviticus 24:20. Many biblical commentators contend that the *lex talionis* was not an "expression of vengeance but a limitation on measureless vengeance."[42] Dante's use of the *lex talionis*, or *talio* in Italian, follows similar reasoning insofar as the *contrapasso* is meant to be no more and no less than a just penalty for earthly sin or, at least, a "starting point for justice."[43] Moreover, while the biblical *lex talionis* was a literal retribution, the infernal *contrapasso* is neither literal nor exact but rather symbolic or metaphysical. Thus, the denizens of the *Inferno* suffer unending, unique punishments for their past offenses.

Several commentators have pointed out that while the *lex talionis* permeates the *Inferno*, "there is no hierarchy of intensity or variance worked out in the seriousness of punishments between differing crimes."[44] In other words, the punishments do not become more severe as Dante descends the *bolge*. Is Brunetto's fate of incessant movement worse than Farinata's entombment in a fiery sepulchre? Does Master Adam, who must endure eternal thirst, suffer more than Pier della Vigna, who was once a man and now is turned into a tree? The answer is no, although in all four instances, the first characters dwell in lower circles than the second.[45] John Freccero, the literary critic, appears to concur with this analysis when he says that "the punishments in hell have little to do with moral theology and almost nothing with the theology of pain."[46] Rather, he says, they are examples of poetic justice and aesthetic appropriateness: the punishments fit the crime. "Whatever the moral theology of the *contrapasso*," Freccero goes on to say, "at the level of representation, it is above all ironic wit."[47]

The very symbolic nature of the *contrapasso* makes it possible for us to accept Pier della Vigna becoming a tree, Ulysses consumed by flame, or Farinata within his eternal sepulchre. Not so the punishments apportioned in the real world, in our post-Holocaust world, where some of the guilty were put to death, some imprisoned, some ignored, some let free, and some rehabilitated and reabsorbed into society.[48]

What are the demands of justice today, and how can we meet them? No one answer is possible, and certainly not in this forum. When Supreme Court Justice Potter Stewart, ruling on pornography, declared, "I know it when I see it," he could have been expressing the common view of justice.[49] Justice derives from fairness, and fairness is a concept within the everyday realm of human experience. Primo Levi also knew justice when he saw it. It spoke to his sense of fair play. That is why his books rue the fact that, in the aftermath of the Holocaust, justice often has yet to be done.

Before we leave the subject of justice, it would be useful to return briefly to the subject of Elias the dwarf in order to reintroduce Levi's thoughts on justice and revenge. As mentioned above, Elias was a campmate who choked Levi almost to the point of unconsciousness after Levi attempted to return a blow he received (the one such time he reports ever having done so). Levi uses the story of Elias and their fistfight to introduce his thoughts on who should render justice. He concludes, as mentioned above, that justice should be left to the "professionals":

> PL: Only because I don't feel I'm capable [of exacting revenge]. Then again, in our civilization, revenge is not allowed, and rightly so.
>
> RS: And yet the desire for revenge is very common.
>
> PL: Yes, the desire for revenge is very common, but to exact revenge is illegal. Now, because of an intrinsic weakness of mine or because of a gap in my upbringing, I'm not capable of acting like Jean Améry.[50] Améry says that, under cover of a bombing raid, he punched a Polish prisoner. Later, he was beaten quite badly because of it, but that was part of his moral code, the *Zurückschlagen*, to render a blow for a blow. I've hinted that Améry probably sentenced himself to death with his *Zurückschlagen* because he was an extremely polemical man. He was polemical with everyone, including me. I didn't mention this in *I sommersi e i salvati*, but some of the letters he wrote to a mutual friend of ours were harshly critical of my stand vis-à-vis the Germans. He considered me a "forgiver," a *Verzeihende*. He wrote a letter saying, "I don't agree with Primo Levi, who tends to forgive everyone a little." That isn't true.[51]

These words reprise Levi's statement in *I sommersi e i salvati*,

> Non ho tendenza a perdonare, non ho mai perdonato nessuno dei nostri nemici di allora, né mi sento di perdonare i loro imitatori in Algeria, in Vietnam, in Unione Sovietica, in Cile, in Argentina, in Cambogia, in Sud-Africa, perché non conosco atti umani che possano cancellare una colpa; chiedo giustizia, ma non sono capace, personalmente, di fare a pugni né di rendere il colpo.[52]

Dispensing pardons is clearly neither desirable nor posssible for Levi. It is similarly extraneous to Dante and the *Inferno*, where the imprisoned sinners are destined to suffer for all eternity; the only place where punishment is considered remedial and pardon is therefore possible is in *Purgatory*.[53]

The concept of *Schadenfreude* introduced earlier may, by contrast and comparison, help us elucidate Levi's stand with regard to both pardon and revenge. To a great extent, repentence is of no account to Primo Levi. He adheres to a strict interpretation of the *lex talionis*, although he does not approach it in a Christian or even Judeo-Christian context. Levi bases his views on justice from his observations and experiences of suffering during the Holocaust, considering a person's duty to society and oneself rather than to a higher religious ideal. Levi is concerned with such moral dilemmas as the conflict between an ethical order and the natural love of self, as well as the unique interpretation of justice that evolved within the barbed-wire fences of the *Lagers*. However, even if taken out of the context of an extreme experience and transported to the level of theory, we would still find Levi's views of justice relatively unaltered. He has stated many times, in books and interviews, that the oppressor should suffer, and that if he suffers, that is just; that the victim should not suffer, and that if he suffers, that is unjust:

> Since I'm not a believer, I don't really know what forgiveness is. It's a concept that's outside my world. I don't have the authority to bestow forgiveness. If I were a rabbi, maybe I would; if I were a judge...I believe that if someone has commited a crime, he has to pay. It's not up to me to

say, "I exempt you from punishment." The authority does not rest with me. I don't say so out of anger, because even when incidents don't involve me directly, like with the Italian terrorists, for example, or even with the repented terrorists, I can't bring myself to forgive them. If they commited a crime, then they have to pay because justice doesn't exist if there's no payment. In *I sommersi e i salvati*, I mentioned the story of the onion–do you remember Dostoyevski's story of the onion? In *The Brothers Karamazov*, Grušenka tells the story of a hateful old crone who, once in her life, gave a little onion to a beggar. After she dies and goes to hell, an angel comes down and reaches out to her with a little onion in his hand. She hangs on to it and is thus delivered from hell. That's a very poetic story, but indefensible. One little onion is not enough. Höss, the commandant of Auschwitz: think of how many little onions he gave away–to his wife, his children, his dog, his horse! He was full of little onions![54]

Let us now turn our attention to an interesting aside contained in *Se questo è un uomo*. We know from the date of the work that, with the possible exception of *Shema* or other poems, *Se questo è un uomo* was the first thing Levi wrote upon his return from Auschwitz. We also know from Levi's introduction to *Se questo è un uomo* that the chapters were written not in logical succession but in order of urgency. Therefore, how urgent is this "aside" we can only judge by its location in the first chapter of Levi's first book after Auschwitz. He says:

> Nei riguardi dei condannati a morte, la tradizione prescrive un austero cerimoniale, atto a mettere in evidenza come ogni passione e ogni collera siano ormai assenti, e come l'atto di giustizia non rappresenti che un triste dovere verso la società, tale da potere accompagnarsi a pietà verso la vittima da parte dello stesso giustiziere. Si evita perciò al condannato ogni cura estranea, gli si concede la solitudine, e, ove lo desideri, ogni conforto spirituale, si procura in-

> somma che egli non senta intorno a sé l'odio o l'arbitrio, ma la necessità e la giustizia, e, insieme con la punizione, il perdono. Ma a noi [the inmates at Auschwitz] questo non fu concesso perché eravamo troppi, e il tempo era poco, e poi, finalmente, di che cosa avremmo dovuto pentirci, e di che cosa venir perdonati?[55]

Keeping the issues of revenge and pardon in mind, a simple gloss of this paragraph would lead us to conclude that Levi denies forgiveness to his former oppressors just as they had once denied it to him. This is an unsatisfactory interpretation for two reasons: one, because as the last sentence of this excerpt makes clear, Levi considers the issue of pardon quite beside the point, since the victims had committed no crime for which to be "pardoned." Two, this reasoning is unsatisfactory because it smacks too much of facile revenge, a puerile tit-for-tat inappropriate to a man who has already told us that "in our civilization, revenge is not allowed, and rightly so."

Then again, this short paragraph juxtaposes paired concepts that reach to the heart of any discussion of revenge: hate and arbitrariness, necessity and justice. Revenge springs from hate and arbitrariness and, as such, is unacceptable; necessity and justice, on the other hand, are indispensible moral imperatives. Why then, moving on to the last paired concepts explored in the above paragraph, why cannot punishment lead to pardon in Levi's schema? No pardon is possible, Levi advances, because (1) a crime has been committed and *chi sbaglia paga*; (2) the crimes were committed with volition, and *mens rea* is at the base of punishment; and (3) the crimes were committed with the excess zeal of *Schadenfreude*, and forgiveness can not assuage that offense.

Aristotle, as paraphrased by Gilbert, wrote that justice is not like the other virtues, in that it is a mean between two extremes of the same vice (injustice) and not, as usual, a property in which vice pertains to one extreme and virtue to the other.[56] Justice, in other words, is the mean activity between acting unjustly and suffering unjustly. Dante's sinners acted unjustly, causing others to suffer unjustly. Now, through their divinely-inspired *contrapasso* in the *Inferno*, justice is done. Levi, on the other hand (and the other innocent victims like him), did not act unjustly but suffered unjustly; his persecutors acted unjustly yet, to a great extent, did not (and do not) suffer at all. Dante and Primo Levi show many thematic and philosophical affinities in their separate handlings of justice. Yet perhaps herein lies the biggest contrast between these two poets of the inferno: Dante's construct, since literary, is complete, while Levi's discourse, since literal, awaits completion.

CHAPTER II

NEITHER *IN BONO* NOR *IN MALO*:

THE GREY ZONE AND THE NEUTRAL SINNERS

In introducing his chapter on the grey zone in *I sommersi e i salvati*, Levi points out that it is human nature to want to simplify, but that "while the desire for simplification is justifiable, simplification itself in many cases is not."[1] He continues:

> Ora, non era semplice la rete dei rapporti umani all'interno dei *Lager*: non era riducibile ai due blocchi delle vittime e dei persecutori. In chi legge (o scrive) oggi la storia dei *Lager* è evidente la tendenza, anzi il bisogno, di dividere il male dal bene, di poter partegeggiare, di ripetere il gesto di Cristo nel Giudizio Universale: qui i giusti, là i reprobi.[2]

In the world of the *univers concentrationnaire*, it was difficult in many cases to decide just who were the victims and who were the oppressors.[3] In the *Lager*, there was not always a clear distinction between the two camps. The dark space between good and evil was often filled with what Levi calls "base and pathetic creatures... [who] sometimes possessed both qualities at once."[4] Much as Dante set aside a special place in hell for the neutral angels who "were not rebels, nor faithful to God, but were for themselves," so Levi has set aside a "grey zone" for collaborators, low-level functionaries, and prisoner-guards. Both of these categories warrant our attention, as does a third, which I will call the *zona dei sommersi* after Levi's latest book; if oppressive non-oppressors fall into a "grey zone," as Levi advances, then their soulless living victims ("i sommersi") fall into a similar limbo of their own. Only a "schematic rhetoric," Levi says, would deny the existence of such creatures or question their peculiarly bivariant nature.

Freccero points out in his book *The Poetics of Conversion* that, according to fourteenth-century tradition, Canto I of the *Inferno* was seen as a prologue to the entire poem, Canto II as a prologue to the *Inferno*, and the poem proper was said to begin only with Canto III.[5] This last canto opens with the fiery message of the gates of hell—*Lasciate ogni speranza, voi ch'entrate* (uncannily reminiscent of *Arbeit Macht Frei*, the equally nefarious language on the gates of Auschwitz). Upon nearing the gate, Dante hears

> Diverse lingue, orribili favelle
> parole di dolore, accenti d'ira
> voci alte e fioche...
> (*Inferno* III, 25-27)

(again, how reminiscent of Auschwitz!) and asks his Master, "che gent' è che par nel duol si vinta?"[6] They are what is known as the "neutral angels," and though Freccero says that they merit "no more than a glance from the pilgrim before he passes on," it could be argued to the contrary that they engage Dante's careful attention.[7]

Virgil explains that these souls are the first class of the lost–humans and angels who "take no risk either of suffering in a good cause or of scandal in a bad one":[8]

> ...Questo misero modo
> tengon l'anime triste di coloro
> che visser sanza 'nfamia e sanza lodo.
> Mischiate sono a quel cattivo coro
> de li angeli che non furon ribelli
> né fur fedeli a Dio, ma per sé foro.[9]
> (*Inferno* III, 34-39)

They are not only *for* themselves, but, as Freccero points out, they are also *by* themselves.[10] Indeed, they are relegated to an infernal locus outside the circular boundary of the River Acheron, isolated even from Limbo. Sinclair puts it thus: "[they] are of no account to the world, unfit for Heaven and barely admitted to Hell."[11]

As we shall see later, the general problem of moral theology in Dante's day is also the problem of the survivor in our age: how to reconcile the "either/or of traditional ethics with the 'natural' love of self?"[12] In other words, how is one to be just unto oneself and yet justly serve mankind? An overweening *amor proprio* can easily lead to injustice toward others; at the same time, excessive attention to the needs of others can lead one to neglect the obligations of *amor proprio*. The difficult balance among these often contrasting ideals is clearly illustrated by Dante. He condemns the violent against themselves to some of the most frightening punishments in the *Inferno*. Yet, Pier della Vigna's fate in Canto III is no more horrible than the pains suffered by either the two spendthrifts or the unnamed suicide at the end of the Canto, whose crimes were much less against their bodies than against their good names, their houses and their families. Clearly, physical harm is not Dante's sole criterion for condemnation; equally important are crimes against the "natural love of self."

How then can we reconcile these seemingly overlapping areas: faithfulness to traditional ethics and justice unto oneself? Greco-Thomistic theoreticians, Freccero points out, maintained that it was in the rational creature's nature to love itself "and that such love could be sinful or just, depending on whether motivated by right reason or *cupiditas*."[13] He continues, "*Malum est defectus, peccatum est actus* was the formula used by Thomas and his contemporaries to distinguish between simple evil and sinful action."[14]

The same Latin formula, seven hundred years later, cuts neatly to the heart of Primo Levi's contemporary neutral locus, the "grey zone." In it, he houses all those who shared complicity in the Holocaust—the collaborators, the *prominents*, the functionaries, the beneficiaries of *protekcja* (protection), the *Kapos*, the *Sonderkommandos* ("special squads" of prisoners in charge of the gas chambers and crematoria), the prison doctors, the Chaim Rumkowskis in the Lodz ghetto and elsewhere.[15] These were men and women whose natural love of self became an overweening love of self. They turned their back on a moral, ethical order and gave in to the evil within themselves.

Levi is careful to advance a partial exoneration on their behalf. Until one is faced with the experience of the *Lager* or the ghetto, he writes, one clings to the atavistic notion that the world may be terrible but always decipherable. We blindly believe in a certain "we-ness" that is inside us, and the "other-ness" which is outside—one being friend, the other foe, and both being separated by a clear "geographic" boundary. The *Lager*, though, brings with it a deep surprise: it is a terrible world but also an indecipherable one. Didn't Clausner (a character in *Se questo è un uomo*) sum it up when, unlike the other prisoners, who etched their tatoo numbers or names on the bottom of their soup bowls, he placed the words *ne pas chercher de comprendre*? The *Zugang*, or new inmate, rapidly learned—to his terror and, in a few diabolical cases, delight—that yes, the enemy was all around him but also inside him. The boundary began to crumble. In a world removed from the world, in an incomprehensible order, what scrap of Judeo-Christian ethics could be of any use? The inmates who discovered the evil within them were often the ones who survived. They were certainly the first to step into the grey zone.

Why doesn't Levi condemn them outright? Why don't these grey zoners take their place with the oppressors? Levi answers this question by saying that he is paralyzed by *impotentia judicandi*.[16] With regard to all the varieties of inmate-collaborators, he states unequivocally that no one—both those who have not had the *Lager* experience and those who have—can be authorized to judge the grey zoners. After unimaginable torment—months of hunger, fatigue, humiliation, death, isolation, and the very "indecipherable inferno" of the concentration camp itself—when offered a chance to survive, who and how many have the reserve of strength to resist?[17] This, Levi says, is the true *Befehlnotstand*, the "state of constriction subsequent to an order," not the wary defense systematically and shamelessly offered by Nazi defendants at war trials, not the weary defense offered by industrialists who capitalized on the forced labor, or justifications given by managers and technicians at Buna and elsewhere.[18] The real *Befehlnotstand* belongs to the victim who, stripped of his dignity and afflicted by the "death of the soul" complies out of injudicious love of self.[19] The difference then between the grey zoners and the neutral sinners is that the former acted while the latter refrained from acting. Nonetheless, these two groups occupy similar niches in their respective infernos since they lived neither *in bono* nor *in malo* but *per sé*.

Thus said, this opening toward a non-schematic, non-dichotomous vision of human nature does not make Levi a moral relativist. "Non vogliamo confusioni, freudismi spiccioli, mobosità, indulgenze. L'oppressore resta tale, e così la vittima: non sono intercambiabili."[20] The Nazis themselves were not unaware of the moral abyss that often separated them from their victims and they devised devious ways to bridge this gap. Perversely, they tried and mostly succeeded in dirtying the hands of their victims with the victims' fellow campmates' own blood. By compromising the guiltless, the Nazis tried to push their own culpability onto their victims, "così [le vittime] avranno contratto coi mandanti il vincolo della correità e non potranno mai tornare indietro."[21]

The extreme example of the Nazi will to compromise their victims was the *Sonderkommandos* (or Special Squads). When composed of German Security Service recruits, as in the Cracow and Warsaw ghettos, the *Sonderkommandos* were responsible for the *Aktionen* that resulted in plundering, deportation, and random massacres of the Jews in the ghettos.

However, when composed of Jewish inmates, as at Auschwitz or Birkenau, the *Sonderkommandos* had an even beastlier job: they were responsible for the functioning and proper managment of the *Lager* crematoria. They were responsible for keeping order among the new arrivals, removing the cadavers from the gas chambers, cutting the women's hair, sorting and classifying clothes, shoes and luggage, transporting the bodies to the crematoria, managing the ovens, and extracting and elminating the ashes.

At Auschwitz, the Special Squad had anywhere from 700 to 1,000 members at any one time. Twelve squads succeeded each other over the life of the camp. Each squad worked for a few months and then was killed; the next squad, as its first task, was charged with burning the cadavers of its predecessor. According to Levi,

> Aver concepito ed organizzato le Squadre è stato il delitto più demoniaco del nazionalsocialismo. Dietro all'aspetto pragmatico (fare economia di uomini validi, imporre ad altri i compiti più atroci) se ne scorgono altri più sottili. Attraverso questa istituzione, si tentava di spostare su altri, e precisamente sulle vittime, il peso della colpa, talché, a loro sollievo, non rimanesse neppure la consapevolezza di essere innocenti.[22]

One day, an extraordinary event occurred in the gas chamber. As the Squad cleared the corpses from the chamber it discovered a young girl, perhaps sixteen years old, buried under a pile of bodies but still alive. The squad worked with death as part of its daily chores and yet, when faced with an individual case, the members found themselves overcome by pity. They revived the girl and a doctor was called in. Just at that moment, SS Commander Muhsfeld happened by. The doctor explained the case to him.

Muhsfeld listened and then decided: the girl must be killed. Loathe to carry out the order with his own hands, he called in an underling who shot the girl with a bullet to the nape of the neck.

In 1947, Muhsfeld was tried for this crime among others, convicted and hanged. Levi comments, "questo fu giusto."[23]

> Non è difficile giudicare Muhsfeld, e non credo che il tribunale che lo ha condannato abbia avuto dubbi; per contro, il nostro bisogno e la nostra capacità di giudicare si inceppano davanti alla Squadra Speciale.[24]

How can they be judged—and who can judge them? There is a middle ground for them in Levi's view, though it is neither decorous nor blameless. The *Sonderkommandos* share the accountability of their overseers, whether their selection for special duty was due to chance, to the effects of *Befehlnohstand*, inherent sadism, frustration, or the "contagion of indentification" spread by the oppressors to the oppressed. Levi concludes, "...chiedo che la storia dei 'corvi del crematorio' venga meditata con pietà e rigore, ma che il giudizio su di loro resti sospeso."[25] These grey zoners thus find themselves in a state of suspended judgment.

Levi reflects that much has been written on the mimesis, identification and exchange of roles between overseer and underling. It is not virgin terrain, he says; on the contrary, it's an overworked field, littered with true, invented, disturbing, banal, acute and stupid pronouncements. He quotes one "field-worker" in particular, Liliana Cavani, director of the film *The Night Porter* (1974), a film which Levi more than once called "beautiful and false."[26] It is a psychological study of a former *Lager* inmate (played by Charlotte Rampling), who takes up with her former guard-rapist-tormenter (Dirk Bogarde) upon meeting him many years later in a Viena hotel. Although she is the wife of a famous conductor and he a night porter, their postwar liason closely replicates the psychological and physical sadomasochism of their concentration camp relationship. In explaining (or perhaps defending) her film, Cavani declared at the time,

> Siamo tutti vittime o assassini e accettiamo questi ruoli volontariamente. Solo Sade e Dostoevskij l'hanno compreso bene...In ogni ambiente, in ogni rapporto, [credo] ci sia una dinamica vittima-carnefice più o meno chiaramente espressa e generalmente vissuta a livello non cosciente."[27]

Levi rejects this formulation outright. He allows that some victims did become assassins and that many victims crossed over into the grey zone but what he does not allow is the formulation expressed by Cavani that the impulse to cross the line rose unbidden and unconsciously from within. "Non mi intendo di inconscio e di profondo," he admits, "ma so che pochi se ne intendono, e che questi pochi sono più cauti; non so, e mi interessa poco sapere, se nel mio profondo si annidi un assassino, ma so che vittima incolpevole sono stato ed assassino no."[28] To confuse victims and assassins, he states unequivocally, is moral sickness, an aesthetistic affectation, a sinister sign. Most of all, Levi warns, it is a precious service rendered voluntarily or not to those who would deny the truth.

The notion of constraint is central to Levi's distinctions among victims, oppressors and that middle ground, the grey zoners; the former are said to join the ranks of the latter upon constraint. To what extent can

Nazi oppressors also claim constraint as the prod for carrying out their orders? A case that illustrates Levi's thoughts on this matter centers on Kurt Waldheim, the current president of Austria and former Secretary General of the United Nations. In 1986, Waldheim was accused of having been a Nazi collaborator and, more specifically, of having assisted the deportation of Greek Jews, Greeks and Yugoslavs to Nazi concentration camps during World War II. When *I sommersi e i salvati* appeared in Italy in the spring of 1986, the Waldheim controversy was in full bloom. Many Italian commentators remarked on the affinities between Levi's "grey zone" and the Waldheim case. In an interview with me a few weeks after *I sommersi e i salvati* was published, Levi said,

> I don't think that Waldheim is technically a war criminal. He was just one of 100,000 others like him. He was a lieutenent with some degree of responsibility. He certainly signed some papers. He certainly lied. He couldn't not have known what was happening at Salonika—it was common knowledge. Certainly he knew, so he lied when he said he didn't. He's a grey zoner! He's a man with a very real responsibility, but one that dwells within the greater responsibility of the Nazi machine.[29]

When asked whether Waldheim had fabricated his own set of truths to shield himself from the past, Levi replied, "Oh, he didn't need to. He's too lucid to need to fabricate a set of truths, don't you think? He certainly is in possession of documents himself. He knows what he did because he was there."[30]

While it would seem from Levi's comments about Waldheim that grey zoners would have no claim to constraint as a means of justifying their actions, at the same time, he also often states that both oppressors and victims were cut from the same cloth. "Erano fatti della nostra stessa stoffa," he says in *I sommersi e i salvati* and earlier, in *Se questo è un uomo*, he writes, "Le SS malvage e stolide, i *Kapos*, i politici, i criminali, i prominenti grandi e piccoli, fino agli *Häftlinge* [prisoners] indifferenziati e schiavi, tutti i gradini della insana gerarchia voluta dai tedeschi, sono paradossalmente accumunati in una unitaria desolazione umana."[31] They have all, however, become "non-men", "non-uomini." "La loro umanità è sepolta, o essi stessi l'hanno sepolta sotto l'offesa subita e inflitta altrui."[32] These grey zoners inhabit a literal "no-man's land."

A third group remains, and they are considered here along with the grey zoners and the victims and oppressors because they are yet a third kind of victim. They are the group that Levi addressed when he asked the question, "Is this a man?" They prove the terrible efficacy of the *Lager* system and suffered Vercor's death of the soul. They are the men whom Levi in *Se questo è un uomo* called "i tristi" and in his latest book calls "i sommersi."

Levi first spoke about this subgroup by way of contrast with his friend Alberto.

> Alberto è il mio migliore amico..."sa" chi bisogna corrompere, chi bisogna evitare, chi si può impietosire, a chi si deve resistere. Eppure (e per questa sua virtù oggi ancora la sua memoria mi è cara) non è diventato un tristo. Ho sempre visto, e ancora vedo in lui la rara figura dell'uomo forte e mite, contro cui si spuntano le armi della notte.[33]

Alberto, therefore, has not become "un tristo," he is still "a man," i.e., he is still alive in terms of morality and human dignity. Many others are not capable of such resistence and are submerged, their spirits annihilated. It is in this context that Levi also gives his clearest acount of the "offense" inflicted on the victims of the Holocaust: the demolition of man (man being understood as vitality, dignity, optimism, identity). There is a cruel double meaning to the term "campi di annientamento," Levi says.

Levi soon learns that, at Auschwitz, his name is "Hundert Vierundsiebzig Funf Hundert Siebzen"–174,517, the number tatooed on his left forearm—yet he insists on scratching his name onto his soup bowl, in the same place that many merely put their numbers. He is known throughout the camp as Primo, or even "the Italian," a name he shares with Alberto. He manages to retain his identity, and at some cost. His campmate Null Achtzehn is not so fortunate. He has no other name besides "018," the last three digits of his tatoo—as if everyone realized that "only a man is worthy of carrying a name and Null Achtzehn is no longer a man."[34] He himself seems to have forgotten his name. He survives as a human shell without a human spirit. Levi comments on "i tristi": "Si esita a chiamarli vivi: si esita a chiamare morte la loro morte, davanti a cui essi non temono perché sono troppo stanchi per comprenderla."[35] These are the "sommersi," the "non-uomini." In one of his darkest moments at Auschwitz, Levi reflects on life "outside." He wonders if it is still beautiful, and he meditates that it truly would be a shame to let himself be "submerged" now. It is interesting to note that he doesn't worry about dying; instead, he seems to imply, to become one of the "sommersi" is a fate worse than death.

There are two people in *Se questo è un uomo* whom Levi explicitly calls "men": Lorenzo and "l'uomo Charles." Lorenzo was the Italian volunteer laborer who provided Levi with the material aid that saved his life (an extra liter of soup a day). His very presence reminded Levi that a just world was possible, that there was a remote possibility that goodness still existed and that maybe the struggle to try to live was worthwhile.[36] Charles was a Frenchman who helped Levi regain his lost humanity in the desperate days before liberation by working with him to help others. By helping others, Levi and Charles were able to save themselves.

But there is yet another "man" in the book—a self-proclaimed man whose final cry reflects further on the theme of justice and injustice as Levi and Dante see them. Towards the end of Levi's internment, he and the other prisoners were marched to the *Appelplatz* to witness a public hanging. The month before, one of the Birkenau crematoria was blown up and the man standing before them, a member of the Birkenau *Sonderkommando*, would die for the crime. One of the German guards made a speech denouncing the crime to the assembled prisoners and ended it with "Habt ihr verstanden?" ("Have you understood?"). Levi remarks that "all and no one" in their "damned resignation" responded "Jawohl." But if no one was aware of answering the guard, all were suddenly made aware of the last cry of the prisoner. "Kamaraden, ich bin der Letzte!" he cried—"Comrades, I am the last!" That there was no reaction from the "abject flock" before him only proved the prisoner's point: he was the last among them, the last "man."[37]

We may be tempted to ask, where are the "sommersi" in Dante? Although Levi's term "sommerso" comes directly from Dante, Dante's organizing structure left no place for Levi's sort of spiritual death. In fact, even the souls condemned to eternal suffering, those guilty of a lifetime of sin and debauchery, nonetheless spring to life upon seeing the River Acheron and the gateway to hell—a fact that surprised Dante himself. Virgil explains that even the lost are so spurred by divine justice "sì che la tema si volve in disio."[38]

There is, however, another sort of link between Levi and Dante. The very description "sommersi" literally comes from the *Inferno*:

> Di nova pena mi conven far versi
> e dar matera al ventesimo canto
> de la prima canzon, ch'è d'i sommersi.
> (*Inferno* XX, 1-3)

The *Inferno* is also rich with images of spirits submerged in swamps, in boiling blood, in ice, in a boiling pond; or feet-up in a stone jar; or swimming through pitch. So, while there is no precise correspondent to Levi's concept of the submerged, his choice of name is undoubtedly Dantesque.

The *Inferno* also has its "non-uomini," although, upon analysis, one must conclude that, like the "sommersi," they cannot be called direct antecedents of the "non-uomini" we have seen in Levi's works. These Dantesque "non-uomini" are variously called "i sommersi" or "i tristi," both terms that Levi has applied to the non-men of the concentration camp universe. In the *Inferno*, we see these creatures in such cantos as VII and

XIII. In Canto VII, Dante encounters souls who are submerged in a black mire and can only gurgle their words.

> Fitti nel limo, dicon: "Tristi fummo
>   ne l'aere dolce che dal sol s'allegra,
>   portando dentro accidioso fummo:
> or ci attristiam ne la belletta negra."
> (*Inferno* VII 121-124)

At first, they might seem to parallel Levi's own group of "tristi," the precursors, as it were, to the submerged. However, close analysis proves the fundamental fallacy of this conclusion. When we learn that these souls are condemned for wrathfulness, that they are "sullen" rather than "sad," and that their states of mind range from choleric to bitter to ill-tempered, they lose all similarity to the hollow "non-uomini" of Levi's works.[39]

Pier della Vigna and his ilk are also described in the *Inferno* as "non-uomini" in the most literal sense: "Uomini fummo, e or siam fatti sterpi," he says.[40] Like the wrathful in Canto VII, Pier della Vigna, too, is condemned for his violent action (in this case, suicide), not his base state of inaction (characteristic of the "tristi" in *Se questo è un uomo* or the neutral sinners in the *Inferno*). Therefore, if we are to compare Dante's *Inferno* to Levi's works, we must confine ourselves to the strict parallels between the neutral sinners of Canto III and the grey zoners in *I sommersi e i salvati*.

How does the notion of will and constraint play itself out in Canto III? It has been mentioned above that the importance of volition in the *Inferno* is shown in part by the fact that the incontinent sinners (i.e., those with the most tenous will) are place in higher (i.e., "better") circles than the dispassionate, or "cold-blooded", sinners. But we still have not considered the question of what consequences the lack of volition has on the neutral sinners of Canto III?

First, it is their very lack of will which has prevented them from entering either heaven or hell. After all, they "stood apart," neither taking up one side nor the other so that now, upon their death

> Caccianli i ciel per non esser men belli,
> ne lo profondo inferno li riceve,
> ch'alcuna gloria i rei avrebber d'elli.
> (*Inferno* III, 40-42)

These words, uttered by Virgil, imply that their sin of indifference to both good and evil is so base that, in the inferno, they are considered more vile than even the denizens of the lowest bolgia, who, were the neutral sinners admitted, would "glory over them."[41] All memory of them has ceased and "mercy and justice disdain them."[42] Unlike the other souls huddled outside the city of Dis who eagerly seek out their imprisonment inside hell as crucial to their right to receive justice, the neutrals make no attempt to cross the Styx or to receive their eternal punishment. Once again, in death as in life, the neutrals take no action, standing apart, demonstrating an utter absence of volition.

As regards constraint, Dante does not countenance the concept of any sort of moral *Befehlnotstand* in his world view, since no amount of constraint could justify a mortal sin. Punishments were meted out in the *Inferno* with no regard for one's fame or worldly reputation. Even a life well-lived could be marred by one unrepented sin, causing characters like

Pier della Vigna or Brunetto Latini to be consigned to the inferno in spite of the tenor of the rest of their lives.

What do these elements—the grey zone, the "tristi" and the "sommersi"—reveal to us about Levi's moral stance? First of all, they reveal the great burden of being a man: one must be true to oneself but also to one's world—and that world, in Levi's case, for a formative period of his life, was Auschwitz. One must protect one's humanity even when it is under siege, because not to do so is to become "submerged." Furthermore, as these examples from Dante and Levi show, there is an abhorrent no-man's land lodged between action/inaction and good/evil, salvation from which takes both strength and will. Humankind, these authors seem to say, lives a precarious equilibrium.

CHAPTER III

OBLIVISCENCE AND REMINISCENCE:

MEMORY AND THE MEMORY OF OFFENSE

> Remember the days of old
> consider the years of many generations;
> ask your father, and he will show you;
> your elders, and they will tell you.
> (*Deut.* 32:7)

With the two words, obliviscence and reminiscence, Philip Boswood Ballard in 1903 undertook the sort of memory study that has largely prevailed since in the social sciences: memory as a physiological entity, a tool, a "muscle" to be tested and exercised.[1] Our approach here begins with this archaic title but will take off in a different direction: memory as knowledge, as justice, as *giustiziere*.

Primo Levi begins his chapter on the "Memory of Offense" in *I sommersi e i salvati* with the words, "La memoria umana è uno strumento meraviglioso ma fallace."[2] Memory is, after all, a physiological function of nerves, blood vessels, oxygen and organic electricity. It is subject to the same wear and tear as any of our other organs: when exercised, like a muscle, it remains vigorous. When neglected, it degenerates. Memory, however, is more than an organic function, much as a mind is more than a brain. Our memory is the repository of the sum of our life experiences. It is the crux of our personality, the crutch on which our future self rests. Without memory, there can be no progress of the human spirit, no possibility that within a single lifetime, or a generation, or a century, past missteps can be retraced and redirected, past wrongs can be recognized and righted.

Memory of this non-physiological kind is crucial to both the *Commedia* and *Se questo è un uomo*. If we are to indulge Dante his literary construct, then the whole of the *Commedia* is the poet's account of the pilgrim's journey (both poet and pilgrim being "played," of course, by Dante). We are to imagine Dante at his writing table near the end of his life recording his memory of a fantastical descent into hell and re-emergence from Paradise made at an earlier point in his life. His tale has little of the present tense, being instead grounded in a past tense as much grammatical as teleological. Not only, but as in a Chinese box, the *Commedia* shows us rememberings within rememberings, as Dante the poet recounts the story of Dante the pilgrim who, during his journey, often looks back on the earlier life of Dante the politican: the past, a more distant past, the most distant past.

What is of interest to us in this study is yet another kind of memory, one of an ultimately grievous and burdensome sort. It is the memory of offense that illuminates the books under consideration herein. In his travels through the inferno, Dante encounters a cackle of sinners, some unknown to him, some immediately recognizable to him. Some of them recognize Dante as well. Yet, almost to a man, they shrink from telling him their stories. Dante cajoles them, tricks them, orders them, shames them into revealing bits of their past lives, their sins and their *contrapasso*. Why is the telling so difficult? Without exception, it is because the memory of the offense is so burdensome, so painful that even the act of speaking of it doubles the bitter sting of the infernal punishment. Memory in a Dantesque context is a sort of punishment; as we shall examine below, it is also a mechanism whereby one of the features that enobles man dehumanizes him as well.

Levi's book *Se questo è un uomo* is a narrative composed from personal experience. Whereas Dante's flight of fancy is so brilliant as to seem utterly real, Levi's scrupulously factual narrative is so bizarre as to seem unreal. Levi does not spare us any of his memories, yet his point is that neither did memory spare him. Survivors, he says, must bear the memory of offense *in aeternum*, much as Dante's shades must bear the memory of their sins. Clearly, though, the difference here is one of justice and injustice: the survivors of the Holocaust are unrelentingly assailed by memory although they were innocent of any sin. Can there be justice in this proposition? Can memory be overcome? These are some of the questions we will try to answer in the following pages by a close reading of *Se questo è un uomo* and *I sommersi e i salvati*, especially in relation to Dante's *Inferno* (and the "noble sinners" and the Ulysses Canto in particular).

To remember, to reminisce, to memorize, to commit to memory, etc.

are just some of the various terms in English that belong to the linguistic group "memory." Nonetheless, according to memory theorist Stanley Munsat, not all the words thus linked are semantic equivalents. In *The Concept of Memory*, Munsat especially distinguishes between the terms "memory" and "remembering." "Memory," he says, implies "a constant state of being, perhaps just below the surface conscious state, that is either present or can be triggered involuntarily and often in spite of the person's will."[3] "Remembering," on the other hand, "indicates a sporadic retrieval, often upon volition ('try to remember'), a view that implies an action that can begin or end."[4]

What Levi seeks to do in *Se questo è un uomo* and *I sommersi e i salvati* is to inculcate a "munsatian" memory as a state of being in all of us: a consciousness of events past that will remain just below the surface. The most important feature of this sort of memory is that it must be permanent, constant, and impervious to the claim "I don't remember." Levi laments that this sort of memory is common only to the victims of the Holocaust, with the tragic result that it thus acts as a *sub-rosa* mental punishment. The memory of offense for Holocaust victims is even more indelible than their blue-green tatoos:

> Ancora una volta si deve constatare, con lutto, che l'offesa è insanabile: si protrae nel tempo, e le Erinni, a cui bisogna pur credere, non travagliano solo il tormentatore (se pure lo travagliano, aiutate o no dalla punizione umana), ma perpetuano l'opera di questo negando la pace al tormentato.[5]

This, to Levi, is a crime. Yet should the memory of these same events find a permanent niche in the *sub-rosa* memories of the non-victims and non-oppressors (those with no direct ties to the Holocaust), then one of the purposes of his repeated teachings would be fulfilled. In such an event, memorylessness would be eradicated; the Holocaust could be analyzed, and eventually understood.

Such non-victims and non-oppressors might be termed "memorizers." According to Munsat, "memorizing is a way of committing to memory, not a form of remembering."[6] Contrary to remembering, it does not require actual experience on the part of the memorizer, but does require "something difficult" as the object. Furthermore, memorizing involves deliberate practice: one may not be able to *remember* Auschwitz, but one can commit the Auschwitz experience to memory. That we do so is the motivation behind Yom Hashoah and Holocaust Memorial Week and various other manifestations, and it is one of Levi's purposes in writing.

Memorizing may be one of Levi's aims in writing, but remembering is his subject. His cast of characters runs from tormentors and oppressors, to "grey-zoners," to victims, all of whom have had the actual concentration camp experience; they have no need to "memorize" it. In fact, if they "try to remember," chances are they will succeed. The obverse proposition is, of course, that the same characters can also use their volition to suppress memory of the past. Levi argues, in fact, that *not* remembering is a choice open to the oppressor. Höss and Stangl, the commandants of Auschwitz and Treblinka, respectively, were inordinately successful at this, as their memoirs and biographies attest.[7] Citing the case of Louis

Darquier de Pellepoix, Commissioner for Jewish Affairs under the Vichy government in France, he says,

> Mi pare di poter ravvisare in lui il caso tipico di chi, avvezzo a mentire pubblicamente, finisce col mentire anche in privato, anche a se stesso, e coll'edificarsi una verità confortevole che gli consenta di vivere in pace.[8]

Just as memory is a subclass of cognition, these tormentors are able to reconstruct the way they know something. In the case of the mass extermination of the Jews, the three men mentioned above—Höss, Stangl, and Darquier de Pellepoix—were able to argue more or less successfully that they knew by rumor, they only knew later, or they did not know at all.

Where Levi would part company with Munsat's theories is over the implication that *victims* can also use their own volition to stop active remembering. In fact, the revolutionary aspect of Levi's writings on the memory of offense lies in the bitter assertion that there is no "remembering" for Holocaust victims, only "memory." They are powerless to stop the flow of their memories; remembering, the "action verb" that began in the death camps, has no end for them. Levi in this regard quotes Jean Améry (the Austrian philosopher mentioned earlier in Chapter II):

> Chi è stato torturato rimane torturato...Chi ha subito il tormento non potrà più ambientarsi nel mondo, l'abominio dell'annullamento non si estingue mai. La fiducia nell'umanità, già incrinata dal primo schiaffo sul viso, demolita poi dalla tortura, non si riacquista più.[9]

To say that, for the victims, life ended with the *Lager* is merely hyperbolic; life continued for them in spite of their past, with their memories of the *Lager* intact as a constant companion, an unwanted *doppelganger*. Some, like Levi, were able to see a bright future ahead of them, even with this spectral presence tugging at their sleeve. Yet the supreme irony is that in a figurative, unjust, and paradoxical sense, life for the oppressors did in many cases end with the *Lager*. They were often able to deactivate the action verb, to stop memory, to retreat from remembering and to find succor in oblivescence. To borrow from the imagery of Dante's *Purgatory* (which we will turn to later in this chapter), they drank lustily of the river Lethe and partook greedily of the river Eunoè.

I sommersi e i salvati has been called a "militant book."[10] Indeed, it militates for understanding, not just of the *Lager*, but also of the survivors of the *Lager* system. Levi begins the book with a puzzling question, "How does the memory of an extreme experience work?" His answer is surprising, if not disconcerting. He begins by asserting that the distinction between good faith and bad faith is often tenuous, as any judge of human nature knows. Given this ambiguity, it is often difficult to judge a criminal, and even more so, a war criminal. The accused will often answer the prosecutor's harangue with "I don't know" or "I don't remember." How are we to interpret that "I don't remember"? Good faith or bad faith? Levi offers a clear explanation, one based on memory:

> Il passato è loro di peso; provano ripugnanza per le cose fatte o subite, e tendono a sostituirle con altre. La sostituzione può incominciare in piena consapevolezza, con uno scenario inventato, mendace, restaurato, ma meno penoso di quello reale; ripetendone la descrizione, ad altri ma anche a se stessi, la distinzione fra vero e falso perde progressivamente i suoi contorni, e l'uomo finisce col

> credere pienamente al racconto che ha fatto così spesso e che ancora continua a fare, limandone e ritoccandone qua e la i dettagli meno credibili, o fra loro incongruenti, o incompatibili con il quadro degli eventi acquisiti: la mala fede iniziale è diventata buona fede.[11]

In short, as the events recede into memory, the accused elaborates on and refines his "convenient set of truths" (*verità di comodo*). The rememberer seeks to become memoryless and usually succeeds; by negating his memories, he rids himself of a hurtful truth, as one would eliminate a parasite from within. Levi's precise comments in this regard closely resemble a passage from Freud's essay on negation, *Die Verneinung*. This should come as no surprise since Levi spoke of having read Freud's works and indeed considered him "a great poet and a man of extraordinary acumen."[12] Freud comments:

> The function of judgment is concerned in the main with two sorts of decisions...Expressed in the language of the oldest—the oral—instinctural impulses, the judgment is: "I should like to eat this", or "I should like to spit it out"; and, put more generally: "I should like to take this into myself and to keep that out." That is to say: "It shall be inside me" or "it shall be outside me." As I have shown elsewhere, the original pleasure-ego wants to introject into itself everything that is good and eject from itself everything that is bad. What is bad, what is alien to the ego and what is external are, to begin with, identical.[13]

Levi mirrors these comments with his own statement:

> Come caso limite della deformazione del ricordo di una colpa commessa, c'è la soppressione...Il memore ha voluto diventare immemore e ci è riuscito: a furia di negarne l'esistenza, ha espulso da sé il ricordo nocivo come si espelle un'esecrazione o un parassita.[14]

Conversely, much as the true guilty parties eventually succeed in fabricating their own revisions of the past, the innocent victims' memories will not permit them to flee. We recently saw an example of this unfold in the courts of Israel a few years back: more than one witness to John Demjanjuk's alleged brutality in the Polish concentration camp of Treblinka testified that he could not forget the walk, the look, the laugh of the former guard. Pinchas Epstein and Eliyahu Rosenberg, two of the prosecution witnesses, swore that Demjanjuk's face invades even their nightly dreams. Their memories, much as they would like to suppress them, will not let them forget.

In the world of the concentration camp, where a lifetime could be consumed in two days and a month in the camp entitled the survivor to the title "vecchio" ("Oldtimer"), only a few days were necessary make recent memories recede far into the past. Physical deterioration was so rapid that, Levi writes in *Se questo è un uomo*, "quando non ci vediamo per tre o quattro giorni, stentiamo a riconoscerci, l'un l'altro."[15]

Upon arrival at Auschwitz, the Italian *Zugangen* decided to meet every Sunday night in a corner of the camp but, Levi describes, they broke off their habit almost immediately. It was too sad to take a headcount each time, to find fewer and fewer of them still alive, and the ones who were, more and more deformed and squalid. It was too tiring to walk those few steps to the meeting place and, the coup de grâce, "poi, a ritrovarsi, accadeva di ricordare e pensare, ed era meglio non farlo.[16]

In Levi's detached analysis of the concentration camp survivors after the war and through the following decades, he posits the memory of offense rising up to torment them. What this passage from his Auschwitz diary shows is that, in the terribly brief world of the concentration camp, a man alive after fifteen days was already in all respects a survivor.

Levi was imprisoned in Auschwitz along with Alberto (one of the "men" we mentioned in the previous chapter) and Alberto's father. In October 1944, after Levi had been at Auschwitz for nine months, rumors began to circulate about a special *selekcja*. This Latin-Polish hybrid euphemistically stood for mass murder, since those "selected" were sent to the gas chambers.[17] In the face of the big "selection" of October 1944, Alberto and Levi exchanged their fears and thoughts of rebellion and resignation, but none of the comforting lies in which it would have been easy to indulge. Alberto's father, at 45 an "old man," was "selected" and perished immediately in the gas chamber at nearby Birkenau. Levi reports that Alberto changed radically in the few hours after his father's death. He began to give credence to rumors that the Russians were near and, therefore, that that hadn't been a selection like the others. No, he insisted, those selected were headed not for the crematorium but for a special camp for convalescents, and his father would soon return. Of course, Alberto's father was never heard from again; Alberto himself perished in the forced evacuation march from Auschwitz in January 1945.

What is Levi's point in recounting this story both at the end of *Se questo è un uomo* and in *I sommersi e i salvati* (in the chapter on the "Memory of Offense")? It is simply that victims also fabricate their own truths. Just as the line between victim and oppressor is not impermeable, neither is the distinction between the users and misusers of memory. It has been noted, Levi reminds us, that many survivors subconsciously filter their memories, preferring to speak of the truces, of the moments of reprieve, of the bizarre and the offbeat rather than the moments of extreme pain. They may alter or rewrite the past to give their memories some respite. Levi's friend Alberto is a case in point. Moreover, Alberto's mother continued to insist, well after the war's end, that she "knew" why Alberto hadn't come home: he was hidden, she said, in the forest, waiting for an opportunity to make his way home. A year later, her version of his continued absence had changed slightly: he was convalescing in a Soviet clinic, had lost his memory, but was improving and would soon come home. Extrapolating from this case, one can rightly ask, "Which of the two parties has really lost its memory?" Victims or oppressors? Alberto and Alberto's mother? Or the concentration camp officials? Stangl and Höss? Demjanjuk?

Before we too readily construct an analogy between the memory of the victim and the memory of the oppressor, we should heed an admonition from Levi himself: "I due sono nella stessa trappola, ma è l'oppressore, e solo lui, che l'ha approntata e che l'ha fatta scattare, e se ne soffre, è giusto che ne soffra; ed è iniquo che ne soffra la vittima, come invece ne soffra, anche a distanza di decenni."[18] The memory of the offense is relentless and ubiquitous through time. It continues to assail the tormentor (which Levi holds is just), provided he has not escaped into a convenient self-constructed world, and it perpetuates the tormentor's work by denying the victims peace (which Levi holds is profoundly unjust since the victims are usually less successful at denying their past than their tormentors). The survivors of the Holocaust are transformed into *Geheimnisträger,* "bearers of the secret," the awful secret about the destruction of man of which they are unable to liberate themselves.[19]

Turning now to Dante, we shall see that memory is crucial to the *Commedia,* working in several intersecting ways. First, the structure of the poem follows a descent into hell with a slow, enlightening ascent through purgatory to paradise. Dante's "geographic" journey follows a more important spiritual voyage which, for our purposes, we can describe as a painful immersion into present memory (hell), followed by veiled memory of an earlier order (purgatory), and culminating in restored memory/vision of a primordial, prelapsarian world. The aim of Dante the pilgrim and, by extension, of man in general, is thus to regain memory.

How different this is from the memory at work in the *Inferno* proper. There, memory is less lofty, more pedestrian. It is, simply speaking, the type of human, physiological memory that stops short of the metaphysical or the beatific. For his "memory theory," Dante had access to that of the ancient philosophers and medieval theologians studied and debated in his day. Aristotle, Platinus, Galenus, Constantine the African, Augustine, Isidore, Averroës, Avicenna and others have been shown to have had an influence on Dante's conception of memory.[20] Plato, in *Menon* (also known to Dante), holds that memory belongs to the soul, to knowing and to remembering, and so to "call to memory" means to retrieve that which one *seemed* not to know but which instead was merely forgotten. The link between "to know" and "to remember," which we saw applied to the persecutors in the *univers concentrationnaire,* was also present in the Judeo-

Arabic tradition. There, the "internal senses" were divided into imagination (which preserved the "forms" of the common senses or fantasy) and memory (which was the repository of cognition). According to this tradition, memory also acted as mediator between body and soul.

The strong ties between memory and knowledge are important for Dante's sinners, just as they are reprehensive for Levi's oppressors. The inhabitants of the *Inferno* both know and remember the extent of their sins. Like Ugolino, they may be reluctant to replay them or, like Filippo Argenti, they may boast of them, but nonetheless there is an inextricable pairing of memory and knowledge. As Munsat might phrase it, in the *Inferno*, *both* "knowing" and "remembering" are active verbs.

In the first use of memory in the *Inferno*, Dante the poet, writing in the present tense, stops to consider the predicament or state of mind of Dante the pilgrim:

> Ahi quanto a dire qual era è cosa dura
> este selva selvaggia e aspra e forte
> che nel pensier rinova la paura!
> (*Inferno* I, 4-6)

Other examples of memory early in the poem are the famous passage which opens the second canto:

> Lo giorno se n'andava, e l'aere bruno
> toglieva li animai che sono in terra
> da le fatiche loro; e io sol uno
> m'apparecchiava a sostener la guerra
> sí del cammino e sí de la pietate,
> che ritrarra la mente che non erra.
> (*Inferno* II, 1-6)

or when Dante comes face-to-face with Charon in Canto III:

> Finito questo, la buia campagna
> tremo sí forte, che dello spavento
> la mente di sudore ancor mi bagna.
> (*Inferno* III, 130-132)

Dante also occasionally stops to meditate on the events of his past life, for instance when he encounters Farinata, Guido Calvalcante or Brunetto Latini.

Perhaps a more interesting use of memory, however, is the role it plays in Dante's colloquia with several of the sinners in the inferno and how it serves as an instrument to their *contrapasso*. It can be argued, for comparative reasons, that Paolo and Francesca, Pier della Vigna, Farinata, Brunetto Latini, and Ulysses–the characters Glauco Cambon calls the "noble sinners" by virtue of being "drammatically individualized and large than [their sins]"–have less to do with Levi's victims and more to do with his oppressors.[21] They, too, readied a trap and were caught in it. They, too, suffer and it is just that they suffer. While they may bear a secret, it is not the unholy knowledge of how man loses his humanity, but is the vile little secret of their offense against the moral and–in Dante's view–God-given order. They, too, seek recourse to memorylessness to cancel their past sins, but in the *Commedia*, it is Dante the pilgrim, the questioner, and the inquisitor, who brings their painful memories to the forefront of their minds, for, as he writes in *Inferno* XXXIII, 150, "cortesia fu [loro] esser villano."

Memory works in myriad ways for Dante's sinners. In the eighth circle, among the panderers, Dante casts his eyes on a soul who, instead of responding, seeks to conceal himself from Dante's gaze. He is Vendico Caccianemico, a senior contemporary of the poet. Dante forthrightly calls him to attention and pronounces his name. What brings you to such a pass, Dante asks? Caccianemico responds,

> Mal volontier lo dico;
> ma sforzami la tua chiara favella,
> che mi fa sovvenir del mondo antico
> (*Inferno* XIII, 52-54)

Memory is painful to Caccianemico, not however for what he has undergone but for what he has inflicted. If it were not for Dante's "clear words," he would gladly prefer to remain in a memoryless stupor.

What are we to make of the words "il mondo antico?" Caccianemico probably means his old life in Bologna. Perhaps it is a reference to the ancient, pre-Christian world, where sin was not punished by eternal retribution, or even to the perfect world before the fall, where sins such as his were both inconceivable and impossible. We could also advance a hypothesis that Dante's clear words—representative of forthrightness, honesty and plainness of custom—remind Caccianemico of his life before he committed his unrepented sin. Perhaps they refer to a more moral world order and are not unlike official Nazi paeons to the simpler, more wholesome life of the golden, Romantic age of Germany.

Primo Levi and other Holocaust survivors like him were unwillingly and inescapably thrust into the role of *Geheimnisträger*, "bearers of the secret." Can the same be said for the souls in Dante's *Inferno*? They also bear a heavy burden; that cannot be denied. The combination of the punishment inflicted on them through the mechanism of the *contrapasso*, the millenary duration of their damnation, and their awareness of their sins makes them a sad and anguished lot. Through Dante's poetic talent, the reader's heart goes out to them, for we see our wordly struggles, our slips, our human and moral deficiencies mirrored in their tragic offenses and faults.

Perhaps the most poignant words of the *Commedia* are those spoken by Francesca in Canto V. Condemned by her great love and unrepentent of love, with Paolo she floats through hell in eternity. For many centuries, Francesca's "infinitely gentle and tender" tale was read as a sort of treatise on the power of love.[22] Oddly ennough, that fits in nicely with Dante's purpose in recounting it, for he aims to show that if you "abandon yourself for a love that is nothing but love...you are in Hell already."[23]

Neither Francesca nor Paolo seem to suffer the physical torments of other sinners (such as Pier della Vigna, for example, or Bertran de Born). They do, however, suffer a torment of the mind–or memory, if you will– that parallels their original sin of ceding to a nearly non-physical, more properly metaphysical love. Part of their *contrapasso* is the inability to refrain from telling their story, a powerlessness in the face of the "disio" to relive their sin for whomever may request it. Through memory they are punished because, as Francesca so poignantly says,

> ..."Nessun maggior dolore
> che ricordarsi del tempo felice
> ne la miseria...
> (*Inferno* V, 121-123)

The greatest of all the noble sinners is a figure who, while different from Francesca in both crime and punishment, is yet similar to her in several ways. Francesca and Ulysses both provoke the "intimate dramatic identification of the poet himself with a doomed soul."[24] They also reveal an undiminished passion for the locus of their sin and their past lives which make remembrance for them both irresistable and infinitely painful.

In a gesture of respect for Ulysses—a man condemned theologically though revered poetically—it is Virgil, not Dante the pilgrim, who in *Inferno* XXVI addresses "la fiamma cornuta." Thus invoked by his erstwhile chronicler, Ulysses thrashes and writhes upon the wind before he "tosses forth his voice" and his pitiful story. Like Caccianemico, Pier della Vigna, and others, the physical violence that permeates Ulysses' recounting parallels the mental torment involved in remembering. Ulysses' story rivets Dante (and the reader) with its brashness, adventure and demonstrated thirst for knowledge. Freccero speaks of Ulysses' voyage as "a symbolic flight of the soul toward a transcendent truth"—ultimately, the same truth that Dante's pilgrimage seeks to unravel.[25]

Why, then, does Dante condemn Ulysses to such a horrible torment? The reasons are many. First, Dante's moral order allowed no short cuts. Ulysses transgressed upon the limits placed on mortal man by deliberately trespassing into the outer limits of purgatory—"acciò che l'uom più oltre non si metta."[26] Furthermore, he played the tempting serpent to the crew's Adam and Eve, urging them to sin. His great failing lies in "his ambition to pose as a man of great and honorable counsel" so that, far from the exceptional paragon portrayed by the Romantic critics, he is nothing but an "exemplary, ambitious, dissembling pretender to noble counsel," equal to the other filth who share his infernal ditch.[27]

Anguish initially blocks Ulysses' memory of his sins (although once his narrative begins, he is caught up in its adventure and challenge). Like Levi's category of oppressors, he would prefer to foget his past misdeeds. Yet unlike Levi's oppressors, Dante does not grant the sinners the same luxury of oblivion that time, tribunals and our postwar society have allowed many Nazi war criminals. Dante's sinners are forced time and again, at the beckoning of an inquisitive question or, perhaps, even in their infernal solitude, to remember, recollect and rue their past offenses. Here, in Dante's *Inferno*, the memory of the offense doesn't plague the innocent (the way it does in real life) but continues to torment the dead *in aeternum*. One feels that if Levi were to set up his own hellish construct, it would be structured much the same way: after all, he agrees with Dante that it is just that the guilty suffer, and not so the innocent.

The only sort of respite allowed the condemned sinners in the *Inferno* is what Freccero calls "the flight of the soul by means of the interior eye," the Plotinian-*cum*-Ambrosian notion paraphrased by Dante in Canto I, verse 25 ("così l'animo mio, ch'ancor fuggiva," or "so my mind, which was still in flight"; in Latin, *fugiamus animo*, or "let us flee with our minds").[28] We see this briefly at work with both Francesca and Ulysses. For a fleeting instant, absorbed in the telling of their tales, they are both transported back to pleasurable, heroic moments in their earthly lives. Francesca can relive her lover's damning first kiss; Ulysses relives his exhortation to his crew to follow "virtue and knowledge." Inevitably, the force of their present condition comes crashing down on them with the telling, but not before they have tasted a drop of forbidden, forgotten sweetness.

It is only apparently preposterous, then, to think that in the midst of Levi's hellish imprisonment in Auschwitz, he turned to the Ulysses canto for respite from his surroundings. It is spring and Levi had been at Auschwitz since late February 1944. After fifteen days there, he could already say, "Eccomi dunque sul fondo. A dare un colpo di spugna al passato e al futuro, si impara assai presto, se il bisogno preme."[29] When this episode occured in June, he was considered, and considered himself, an "oldtimer," *un vecchio*.

Levi is approached by Jean, a Frenchman, at 24 the *Pikolo* of his *Kommando*, who wants to learn Italian. Levi chose the "textbook"–the Ulysses canto, which he tries to quote from memory. "Chissà come e perché mi è venuto in mente?," Levi asks.[30]

Significantly, Levi begins the lesson with verse 85 ("Lo maggior corno della fiamma antica"), exactly the point in which Ulysses thrashes and writhes at the effort of remembering. Levi, too, writhes under the task of remembering the verses and trying to translate them into French for Jean. "Povero Dante," he says, "e povero francese!"[31] Levi's memory fails him until he gets to the verse, "Ma misi me per l'alto mare aperto." He tries to convey the force of it, the power implied in "misi me" of a man trying to crash through a barrier. He comments that both Jean and he know that feeling well (a reference, of course to the barbed wire barrier around the camp). Could it also be a reference to the protective barrier of memorylessness which allowed the concentration camp inmates to survive by renouncing their claims on both their past and future?

The next salvageable phrase is "acciò che l'uom più oltre non si metta," the prophetic phrase in which Ulysses acknowledges his trespass and seals his fate. Then a blank until Ulysses' famous oration to his crew:

> Considerate la vostra semenza:
> fatti non foste per viver come bruti
> ma per seguir virtute e canoscenza.
> (*Inferno* XXVI, 118-120)

Levi finds this sentiment uplifting, transporting, enobling: "Come se anch'io lo sentissi per la prima volta: come uno squillo di tromba, come la voce di Dio. Per un momento, ho dimenticato chi sono e dove sono."[32] Ulysses' words have the same effect on Levi in Auschwitz that they had on Ulysses in hell: temporary oblivion, the call to a nobler destiny, forgetfulness of present woes. Jean seems moved by them as well, by their message for "all men in travail." Another lacuna, then "...quando mi apparve una montagna, bruna/per la distanza," and Levi is fully immersed in the transport of the words. He sees not Dante's purgatory (as Ulysses did) but his own mountains, lying between Turin and Milan. *Pikolo*, he almost cries out, don't let me think of my mountains! Memory of them would be too devastating.

Once again, Levi draws a blank until the last four lines of the poem. He stops at the words "come altrui piacque," the "so human and necessary and yet unexpected anachronism."[33] While trying to explain those words to Jean, an intuition of why they are at Auschwitz, the meaning of their destiny, flashes across his mind. However, just as Ulysses, who in recalling his greatest human feat inevitably bursts the bubble of soothing memory, so Levi's momentary epiphany comes crashing down around him as the cooks officially announce the day's soup: Kraut und Rüben, cavoli e rape, choux et navets, kaposzta és répak, cabbage and turnips. Levi, like Ulysses, is back in hell: "infin che 'l mar fu sopra noi rinchiuso."

At Auschwitz, the inmate was surrounded by a protective barrier of memorylessness which allowed him to survive by renouncing his claims on both past and future. Levi was different. He left the door of memory ajar. Unlike Ulysses, he didn't try to crash through the barriers that surrounded him (whether physical, like the barbed-wire fences, or metaphysical, like a dulled memory). Yet he slips unwittingly into a past dimension: when quoting from Dante, he returns in his mind to his home in Turin. Perhaps this was Levi's *fugiamus animo*—his flight of the soul by means of his interior eye. By reaching deep into his memory, back to an almost unthinkable time when he was still a university student in Turin, he tries to inject a breath of humanity into his present condition (in this case, the past = humanity, the present = inhumanity).

A persistent doubt may remain in the reader's mind: isn't it possible that the Romantics were right and that Dante was wrong? Can't Ulysses be viewed not merely as a "noble sinner" but as just plain noble? Evidently, Dante is also torn in his judgment. He reveres yet unequivocally condemns Ulysses. Virgil reveres him, yet bows to the Dantesque vision. Levi reveres him yet falls victim to his Circean song. What is Ulysses' fatal flaw that so attracts our fancy? Ulysses, in fact, is one of Dante's finest, most complex creations. He is a man of great breadth of vision who ultimately is undermined by a wealth of flaws. As Cassel points out, he represents a *habitus*: not one overriding sin, but a "habitual, mortal sin arrived at by degrees."[34] Ulysses is undone by his pride, his lack of restraint, his preference for worldly honor over divine and familial obligations. As we have seen in previous sections, *habitus* is one of the preconditions for punishment, and Ulysses suffers punishment through his fiery *contrapasso* in the *Inferno*.

Another tragic figure of the *Inferno*, Count Ugolino, confesses his grief at being forced to recall his crime. Ugolino della Gherardesca, Count of Donoratico, was convicted of political treachery and locked in a tower along with his sons and grandsons. There, they starved to death, with Ugolino being the last to die. He addresses Dante,

>Tu vuo' ch'io rinovell
>disperato dolor che 'l cor mi preme
>già pur pensando, pria ch'io ne favelli.
>(*Inferno* XXXIII, 4-6)

Our attempt at linking Dante to Levi with regard to the memory of offense takes on an added dimension when we mention that Ugolino is the only character from Dante whom Levi mentions directly in his chapter on that topic; in fact, Levi finds Ugolino's reluctance to speak of his tremendous punishment "psychologically credible."[35]

Dante encounters two other minor characters in his journey through hell, both of whom illustrate an aspect of the function of memory in the

Commedia. Pope Nicholas and Pope Boniface, though confined in different *bolge*, are both condemned along with the fraudulent. In Canto XIX, Dante comes across Nicholas planted in the ground head-first like a pole. The former pope begins speaking only under the false assumption that Dante is another (Boniface). When he realizes his mistake, it is too late to take back his words and he reluctantly allows Dante to question him. The mood evoked in this brief exchange is, once again, Dante's earnest curiosity and the sinner's resolve to remain silent. Only with great resignation does Nicholas agree to delve into his past.

Several cantos later (in *Inferno* XXVII), Dante encounters Guido da Montefeltro. Less earnest and more conniving here, Dante urges Guido to speak "se 'l nome tuo nel mondo tegna fronte."[36] Fame, being closely linked to memory, is the bait Dante dangles to entice Guido to speak. Guido complies, but in so doing flatly refuses Dante's promise of undiminished fame: in fact, he makes it clear that he only speaks because he believes Dante, and his words with him, will never reach the world again.

> ...S' i' credesse che mia risposta fosse
> a persona che mai tornasse al mondo,
> questa fiamma staria sanza più scosse.
> (*Inferno* XXX, 61-63)

Neither fame nor memory are Guido's desire: it is instead oblivion that he seeks.

We have seen that use of memory theory gives access to interesting facets of the Holocaust experience—whether that of the victim or that of the oppressor—and that these speak directly to Primo Levi's personal experience and his writing on the "memory of offense." We have also seen that Dante, as poet and as pilgrim, evokes and experiences memory in various ways. Memory is an expository device of Dante the poet, as it was often a crucial component of the *contrapasso* in the *Inferno*. However, in the world of Dante the pilgrim and in the God-ordered realm of the underworld that he traverses, memory frequently transcends metaphysics to become retribution.

Augustine counted *memoria*, along with *intelligentia* and *voluntas*, as one of the three faculties of the soul. Dante, who was well-versed in Augustine's works, reflects that notion and builds on it in Canto XXV of the *Purgatory*:

> Quando Lachesis non ha più del lino
> solvesi da la carne, ed in virtute
> ne porta seco e l'umano e 'l divino:
> l'altre potenze tutte quante mute;
> memoria, intelligenza e volontade
> in atto molto più che prima agute.
> (*Purgatorio* XXV, 83-88)

Memory, Dante seems to say, is much freer to act when it is released from the body by death and belongs only to the soul. Is this a reason why the souls suffer so in hell? Do their newly-released, newly-fortified memories exacerbate the sinfulness they are expiating? These sinners, however, have no hope of salvation: their eternal home is and will be hell. Nonetheless, the pain experienced through remembering is a *necessary* pain in that it is part of their conformity to divine justice.

How do the characters themselves perceive their own fame (or infamy, as the case may be)? How do they react upon hearing from Dante that their names live on in the world above? Almost without exception, they express emotions ranging from chagrin (Guido da Montefeltro) to horror (Count Ugolino). Few are the defiant ones in the *Inferno* who exclaim as one shade does,

> E perché tu di me novella porti
>   sappi ch'i' son Bertram dal Bornio, quelli
>   che diedi al re giovane i ma' conforti.
> (*Inferno* XXVIII, 133-135)

Rather, many sinners admit and rue their crimes. While they must serve their sentences in hell for eternity, suffering mortification of the flesh according to the requisites of their *contrapasso*, it is indeed another sort of mortification, one of the spirit, to learn that their good names have turned to bad, or even that their bad names live on in the world above. Mastro Adam rebukes Sinon the Greek with these words:

> ..."Ricorditi, spergiuro, del cavallo,"
>   rispuose quel ch'avea infiata l'epa;
>   "e sieti reo che tutto il mondo sallo!"
> (*Inferno* XXX, 118-120)

It must be said, however, that not all Dante's sinners shrink from his enticement. Dante says to Griffolino of Arezzo,

> Se la vostra memoria non s'imboli
>   nel primo mondo da l'umane menti,
>   ma s'ella viva sotto molti soli,
> ditemi chi voi siete e di che genti.
> (*Inferno* XXIX, 103-106)

and Griffolino complies without further ado.

In recent times, we have witnessed a similar phenomenon in the Western world. Some ex-Nazis similarly require little prodding to tell their tales—and even ply their trades. Klaus Barbie, the "butcher of Lyons," who reportedly trained a police-run torture squad in Bolivia during his sanctuary there, used an unsuccessful "but France is guilty too" defense during his 1987 trial there. He denied specific accusations of torture, though he did not deny his role as German Gestapo chief in Lyons during the war.

The Klaus Barbies, like the Griffolino di Arezzos, are the exceptions to the rule. The guilty parties in the Holocaust normally shun the spotlight just as the sinners in the *Inferno* tried to ignore Dante's entreaties. The oppressor has nothing to gain by seeking fame, no claim to glory, and often rejects the basis for notoriety. "John" Demjanjuk insisted he was not the "Ivan" Demjanjuk who operated Treblinka's gas chambers; similarly, Karl Linnas, commandant of the Estonian concentration camp at Tartu, also claimed to be a victim of mistaken identity.[37] It is ironic that, during the war, in the Ukraine, in Estonia, in France, or in any corner of the Third Reich, these same men could justifiably have dreamt of fame and glory. Had the Germans been victors, they might have been heroes for the ages instead of just heroes to the Reich. The moral order of Nazi Germany was convoluted enough to engender just such speculation on the part of its bureaucrats and functionaries.

Today, for the oppressors, the heinous nature of their own acts transcends the human imperative to remember, confounds attempts at understanding, and goes against their *amor proprio*. Obliviscence, or the process of forgetting, is their solution of choice. For the most part, they choose not only personal memorylessness, but also shrink from any sort of public renown. Fame, infamy, glory and notoriety are all concepts linked to memory, not in its interior connotation but in its exterior, institutionalized form. All imply the act of remembering, whether to the benefit or detriment of the subject; furthermore, all tap into the collective memory of a generation, a people or a place.

A fascinating case in point is Kurt Waldheim, a man we have referred to above in Chapter II. Levi calls Waldheim a *grigio*–a grey zoner–since he was an aggregate, not a principal, in the Nazi war machine. Investigators for the U.S. Justice Department believe that "Waldheim participated in the deportation of Greek Jews to Nazi death camps in 1944 and helped turn over allied prisoners to the German SS. Nonetheless, he gave the impression that he had been wounded on the Soviet front in 1941 and spent most of the remaining war years finishing his studies."[38] Waldheim, according to Levi, is too lucid to have constructed a set of truths to mask his wartime crimes. At the very least, however, he dissimulated about his past to keep it buried as long as possible and to obfuscate the truth when Jewish groups tried forcibly exhumed it.

What makes Waldheim such a fascinating figure is that he shunned both fame and infamy for his Nazi years, and yet avidly sought fame and glory as a world statesman. He has released many official statements detailing his war-years activities and military duty, and has even published an autobiography in which facts are carefully omitted, transposed or modified. And yet Waldheim's continued search for fame, glory, and renown ultimately led to his public unmasking.

Even Waldheim, it appears, was susceptible to the lure of memorylessness—at least enough to be able to justify to himself and to his followers a career of public service. That he became Secretary General of the United Nations is significant for what it says about his capacity to forget and deceive (and about government bodies around the world). As Dante says in the *Convivio*, "Quanto gli uomini più smemorati fossero, più tosto sarebbero nobili; e per contrario, quanto con più buona memoria, tanto più tardi nobili si farebbero."[39] Waldheim was avid for this sort of *nobilità* and as a result, exemplifies Levi's model of a "grey zoner."

Memory is essential to the sinners assigned eternally to the inferno; as was pointed out above, it is also one of the fundamental underpinnings of the pilgrim's journey in the *Commedia*. Gaining paradise—for Dante, as well as the human soul whose itinerary he represents—means restoring harmony with the divine order and regaining memory of the prelapsarian world. In the ascent through purgatory to the third realm, the relationship between *memoria* and *intelletto* alters as man gets closer to God, as his intellect merges with the divine, and as his faculties increasingly work outside their usual constraints.[40] Ultimately, unable to keep up with the expanding intellect and overwhelmed by the vision of God, memory transcends any capacity for remembering. The impediment to memory is not just the inability to express its contents in human language; it is also the human inability to remember such a "superhuman" experience.

The second cantica of the *Commedia* includes a very important reference to memory, one that we mentioned earlier, and one that is telling both for how Dante conceived the application of memory and for its implications for Levi's "memory of offense" and justice. At the end of *Purgatory*, in Canto XXXIII, Dante drinks first of Lethe and then Eunoé. Lethe, as Singleton explains, "was the traditional river of the lower world from which the shades drank and thereby were granted forgetfulness of the past."[41] Virgil himself mentions it in the *Aeneid* and its name comes from the Greek word for oblivion. Dante first spies it, together with its companion river, Eunoé, on the summit of Mount Purgatory.[42] Eunoé, a word Dante coined from the Greek to mean "well-minded", was said to "restore the memory of good deeds (just as Lethe, which must be drunk first, takes away the memory of sinful deeds)."[43] Moreover, several commentators (with Singleton and Ciafardini being notable exceptions) feel that Lethe is the same "ruscelletto della natural burella" mentioned as Dante us about to leave hell in *Inferno* XXXIV, 130. The implication is that Lethe washes the sins of hell into purgatory where, coupled with Eunoé, it marks the entrance to paradise. In other words, Dante's coupling of Lethe and Eunoé implies that during their ascent through purgatory, sinners enter into a radically positive state of obliviscence where wrong deeds are forgotten and nothing but the memory of good deeds persists. Dante himself partakes of this "dolce ber" as a rite of passage for his journey on to paradise.[44]

When Dante comes upon the Lethe and Eunoé, at first he calls them by biblical names: Tigris and Euphrates, two of the four rivers mentioned in Genesis as springing from the Garden of Eden. The Tigris and

Euphrates are also the two rivers mentioned in Psalm 137 of the Old Testament. Unique among the Psalms in the Bible, the Song of Exile is a call for vengeance on the enemies of Israel: "By the rivers of Babylon," it begins, "there we sat down, yea, we wept, when we remembered Zion."[45] This chain of references from the rivers of memory to the rivers of revenge raises a question of interpretation: by immersing himself in Lethe and Eunoé, is Dante calling on or acknowledging God's powers of vengeance?

One cannot help but feel that the spirit and effect of Dante's "sweet draught" has been appropriated and perverted in the post-Holocaust West. Primo Levi points out that, in our world, access to symbolic Lethes and Eunoés is limited to oppressors and tormentors and denied to victims, that those with the least sin are refused *oblio*, while those with the greatest sin drink furtively and heartily of sweet forgiveness. The key to forgiveness in Dante's world, and the sole path to paradise, was repentance. Lethe, in medieval iconography, was portrayed as springing from Christ's wounds, symbolizing mercy and leading to the Creator. No such charity is evidenced by the high command of Auschwitz. Where is the repentence in the perpetrators of the Holocaust? By fiat, they usurped one more prerogative of their victims. By using their own sort of *intelligentia* and the sheer force of mental *voluntas*, the oppressors circumvented remembrance, washed away their bad deeds, and froze memory of their goods deeds in the waters of the two rivers of Hades.

While the chronological limits of this work on Primo Levi stretch from 1947 to 1986 (the publication dates of *Se questo è un uomo* and *I sommersi e i salvati*, respectively), it is hard to resist arranging Levi's comments, like bookends, on forty years of our history. One of Levi's last works speaks subtly yet directly to the subject of this chapter, memory and the memory of offense. Call *Il disgelo*, it is a brief poem published posthumously in 1987. The last stanza reads,

> Siamo stanchi d'inverno. Il morso
> Del gelo ha lasciato il suo segno, su carne,
> mente, fango e legno.
> Venga il disgelo. E sciolga la memoria
> Della neve dell'anno scorso.[46]

While the last line faintly echoes Villon's famous refrain from *La Ballade (des dames du temps jadis)*—"Mais ou sont les nièges d'antan?"—more importantly, they lie as softly as a snowfall on Levi's forceful, sometimes brutal, always steadfast analysis of memory, the Holocaust, oppressors and victims. Let the victims become untethered from the painful memories, he seems to say; let the memories of the oppressors, frozen in time, thaw into acknowledgment and bloom into justice. Indeed, we are all tired of winter.

CONCLUSION

Primo Levi's apparent suicide on Saturday, April 11, 1987, just two days before the beginning of Passover, sent a shock wave through the Italian Jewish and literary communities. While close friends knew he had suffered bouts of depression over the winter, his death seemed nonetheless to go against the underlying tenets of his books and even the very way in which he lived his life. Some friends still refuse to believe that it was a suicide at all, instead insisting that his five-floor fall down the stairwell of his apartment building was the result of a *malore*, faintness.

Three weeks after Levi's death, his close friend and admirer for over forty years, Rita Levi Montalcini, railed against the speculations about his death from the pages of *Panorama* magazine.[1] Speaking from a position of authority as a friend of the family for over forty years, she wrote, "First of all, we all know that Primo Levi was absolutely against suicide." Morover, she continued, he was against even the notion of an "ethical suicide" tied to the memories of the *Lager*.

Levi Montalcini, herself, like Levi, from Piedmontese Jewish family, does not believe that Levi's death was a suicide at all. Instead, she posits that, still weak from his recent operation and light-headed, he leaned over the railing outside his five-floor apartment and accidentally fell to his death. Levi, after all, she exclaims, was also a chemist: if he had wanted to kill himself, he knew much less painful, less dramatic and surer ways to do it. Levi Montalcini instead feels that, far from the victim of the *Lager*, as the press has suggested, he was instead the victim of momentary faintness.

> ...che messaggio ci sarebbe in quell'uccidersi così di Primo...Un messaggio atroce, orrendo, che distrugge il messaggio di coraggio che ha mandato a tutti noi anche nell'ultimo *I sommersi e i salvati*, un messaggio di che cos'è la capacità di ribellarsi all'obbedienza. Non si può contraddire tutta una vita l'ultimo giorno, l'ultimo minuto. È ripugnante che un suicidio, e di una persona di tale levatura, possa essere ritenuto normale, dovuto. E come tale accettato da tutti per pigrizia mentale. Ma non da me.[2]

As an author, Levi was one of the new generation of Italian writers who most liberated himself from the nineteenth-century way of making literature. By the time of his death, he had earned himself a place in Italian letters and in world literature; he had also become a staunch and much-admired defender of the Italian Jewish community. Perhaps the most lasting memory of Primo Levi nevertheless will be as a human being. He once said of his good friend and author Mario Rigoni Stern, "è raro trovare un legame tra l'uomo che scrive e l'uomo che vive."[3] A man such as Levi—intellectual, chemist, novelist, thinker, a man who was neither moody nor melancholy, a craftsman who prided himself on his deliberateness of action and rationality of thought—would not plausibly commit such an uncharacteristically dramatic act without significant forethought or deep moral anguish.

Friends with whom Levi spoke in the months preceding his death acknowledge that he was despondent over what he perceived as the increasing obliviscence of the Western world, which, in his view, seemed willing to forgive and anxious to forget the events of the Holocaust. Memory had become institutionalized through Holocaust Memorial Days and granite or marble monuments, but it had not become internalized in our collective psyche. The Western world lets the Holocaust recede far into its memory, diminishing and redimensioning it until one pesky world event or another brings it back to the surface: Demjanjuk on trial in Jerusalem, Linnas deported to Lithuania, Waldheim placed on the U.S. Immigration "Watch List," and Barbie captured in Bolivia. Even more to the point, burgeoning revisionist fringes and mainstream apologists in the United States, France, Germany, and even Italy appear determined to prove "scientifically" that the Holocaust never happened. Were Levi's words in vain? Did his indefatiguable lecturing, writing, speechmaking, and publicizing fall on deaf ears and closed minds? Were these the thoughts that crossed his mind as he fell to his death?

Primo Levi's primary concern, at least in his last book, is the intersection of memory and justice. He argues on an individual level that lack of memory is a form of injustice (in the oppressor), while full memory in those same individuals results in the possibility of justice; at the same time, he argues, full memory in the death camp survivors is an unending torment. A political cartoon about the Barbie trial in France neatly illustrates the tie between memory and justice. In it, a young man asks an older one, "It's been more than forty years. Why are we hunting down a bunch of pathetic old men just to prosecute them for...er...uh...well, you know...uh...whatever that stuff was they did...? The older man answers, "That's *precisely* why."[4] Unless the collective memory of the acts of genocide and murder committed during the Holocaust is kept alive, it becomes impossible to "do justice" according to even the most restrictive legal interpretations, i.e., to bring to trial those accused of committing a crime. Put differently, this means that if we forget, justice may wither from lack of exercise.

Primo Levi's comments vis-à-vis memory are pertinent here: "È certo che l'esercizio [...] mantiene il ricordo fresco e vivo, allo stesso modo come si mantiene efficiente un muscolo che viene spesso esercitato."[5] Even the names of Holocaust memorial organizations have begun to reflect a concern with active memory (as opposed to the "passive memory" expressed through placques, medals or monuments). The Foundation for Future Generations takes its name from a concern that memory be nourished and preserved; a 1988 international conference, sponsored in part by the U.S. Holocaust Commission, also summed up this active concern in its concise name, "Remembering for the Future."

Memory, however, is no one's exclusive domain. At the same time as Jewish and ecumenical groups attempt to protect memory for the future, an antithetical Russian nationalist organization is using memory to revive some of the very spectres of the past that contributed to the Holocaust. Called *Pamyat*, or "Memory" in Russian, this grass-roots organization supports a politcal agenda that includes denunciation of rock musicians as purveyors of satanism and devotion to Tchaikovsky and Dostoevsky.[6]

That, however, is just its more eccentric, Russophile side. More alarming, *Pamyat* also sees the "Russian homeland" as beset by enemies, chiefly "International Zionism" and Fremasonry. These same claims were advanced eighty years ago in a notorious Czarist forgery, *The Protocals of the Elders of Zion*. In the thirties, the Italian Fascists employed accusations of international Zionism and Freemasonry ultimately to justify enactment of racial laws in 1938. The same accusations also spurred the Nazi Party in Germany to develop theories of genetically-derived "racialism" to separate, legislate against, and eventually annhilate millions of Jews. How ironic that, at a time when some of the last living war criminals are finally coming to trial, a Russian group is reviving the charges that in part led to their crimes–and all in the name of "memory."

Levi spoke in *I sommersi e i salvati* of how the oppressors and persecutors of the Holocaust strove through subtle psychological processes to negate their memories of past deeds and to elaborate instead "convenient sets of truths." In language similar to Freud's, Levi speaks of their desire to eliminate this parasite–their memory–from within. Levi himself calls for undiminished, unadulterated memory, but he does not make a case for the enshrinement of memory.

In *Il giardino dei Finzi-Contini*, Giorgio Bassani, another Italian-Jewish writer of Levi's generation, shows his fascination with memory and its importance in a historical context. Its central characters celebrate a cult of memory, even going as far as to say:

> ...anch'io, come lei, non disponevo di quel gusto istintivo
> delle cose che caratterizza la gente *normale*. Lo intuiva

> benissimo: per me, non meno che per lei, più del possesso delle cose contava la memoria di esse, la memoria di fronte alla quale ogni possesso, si sa, non può apparire che delusivo, banale, insufficiente. Come mi capiva! La mia ansia che il presente diventasse *subito* passato, perché potessi amarlo e vagheggiarlo a mio agio, era anche sua, tale e quale. Era il *nostro* vizio, questo: d'andare avanti con la testa sempre voltata all'indietro. Non era così?[7]

Their world is all backward-looking, perhaps because their future as Italian Jews in 1939 was inescapably bleak. Levi, in contrast, was radically forward-looking, convinced that only a clear view of the past could enable an appreciation of the future. Ultimately, perhaps, a naggingly bleak view of our future cast a shadow over the joy and optimism that most readers found expressed even in Levi's harshest books.

Another story by Bassani may afford more insight into Levi's life and death. *Una lapide in Via Mazzini* tells the tale of concentration camp survivor Geo Josz and his sudden reappearance in Ferrara in August 1945, just as the Jewish community is mounting a wall plaque to commemorate the Ferrerese deportees who died in the Nazi death camps.[8] Josz is horrified to find his name among the 183 victims. The plaque will have to be modified, he says, or redone.

Josz soon takes up his old life, his old natty clothes, his old habits. He is silent about Buchenwald and no one shows any interest in questioning him. For two years, he lives his life as before until a public altercation with a former Fascist spy shatters his reserve. After a lively exchange just out of hearing of a group of friends, Josz slaps the former spy hard on the cheeks. He returns to his house and dresses anew in his concentration camp rags. He begins to speak of his Buchenwald experience in a torrent of words that threatens never to stop. Both Jews and Gentiles are accosted by Josz but neither group pays him any heed. For two years, he continues his tirade, hoping to be a living testimony and yet impressing his tale on no one. One day, Josz realizes his efforts are in vain. He disappears from Ferrara, never to be seen again.

Levi also made a sudden reappearance on the world scene, with the republication of *Se questo è un uomo* in 1957 (the first edition had come out in 2500 copies in 1947, the 600 remainders of which sat forgotten in a warehouse until the great flood of Florence destroyed them in 1966). Levi, too, told his Auschwitz story over and over, for the next thirty years. I asked him 1986,

> RS: At the beginning of *I sommersi e i salvati*, you quote from *The Rime of the Ancient Mariner*:
>
>> Since then, at an uncertain hour,
>> That agony returns;
>> And till my ghastly tale is told,
>> This heart within me burns
>> (vv. 582-85).
>
> After reading that, I wondered, is it ever possible to stop "telling?"
>
> PL: You read the answer in that same book. Some of my friends, dear friends at that, never speak of Auschwitz at all. Others talk about it incessantly, and I'm one of them. I exaggerated a bit when I quoted Coleridge. My heart isn't constantly burning. Many years have passed and, above all, I've written many books on the subject, I've given a huge number of talks in schools and at conferences, and I've talked with a tremendous amount of people.

All this has built up a sort of diaphragm, a barrier, so you can say I was really a bit rhetorical in quoting Coleridge.

RS: It's a beautiful passage!

PL: I know! I was struck by it when I first read it. I was struck by this fact in particular: if you remember the scene of the Ancient Mariner, he grabs the weddings guests, who pay him no heed–they have the wedding on their minds– and forces them to listen to his tale. Well, when I had just come back from the camp, I acted in the same way. I had an impelling need to tell this story to whomever at all! I had just gotten a job as a chemist in a little paint factory near Turin and the workers there considered my something of a harmless kook because I did the exact same thing: I told my story to anyone and everyone, at the drop of a hat, from the plant manager to the yardman, even if they had other things to do–just like the Ancient Mariner. And then I would type into the night (because I also lived in the factory). I typed every night and this was considered even crazier!

RS: And what was their reaction to your story?

PL: It was...correct. I don't know. They listened, some were even very interested.

RS: Did you tell your story in spite of yourself or with the precise idea that you had to tell it?

PL: I really needed to tell it. Now, if you ask me *why* I needed to tell it, I'd have a hard time answering you. But I had the feeling that I think Catholics must have when they go to confession: it's a great relief to confess. Or the feeling you have if you're in therapy with a psychoanalyst and by telling your story, you break free of it. But there's more to it than that. A very intelligent friend of mine once said to me, "That period was in Technicolor and the rest of your life has been in black and white." And that's pretty close to the truth.[9]

Levi remarks, in a passage that takes on added significance since his alleged suicide, that one of the most dangerous mental passtimes for the concentration camp inmates was to think of the past while in the camp; later, the danger came from reliving their camp experience. Levi says, "Credo che proprio a questo volgersi indietro a guardare 'l'acqua perigliosa' siano dovuti i molti casi di suicidio dopo (a volte subito dopo) la liberazione."[10] From what we have seen in our examinations of justice, of the grey zone, and of memory, we can say with some confidence that it is equally dangerous *not* to look back at the "acqua perigliosa" now that the Holocaust is past. Levi calls for unflagging vigilance in his books; he asks that justice be served or, should that prove humanly impossible, that it at least be cherished and remembered, like "a sign upon our hands."

The three topics treated above—justice, the grey zone/the neutral angels, and the memory of the offense—reveal striking interplay between ideas formulated by Dante seven hundred years ago and ideas advanced by Primo Levi in this century. Not all of their interpretations of these concepts mesh, and certainly their approaches to similar topics more often than not are divergent rather than convergent. However, it is striking that both writers did in fact touch on many of the same issues and made these issues central to their works. The Auschwitz experience can undoubtedly be read as a modern-day inferno. Does that make Primo Levi a Dante of our time?

NOTES

INTRODUCTION

¹For a discussion of Dante's place in contemporary Italian arts and letters, see Zygmunt G. Baranski, "The Power of Influence: Aspects of Dante's Presence in Twentieth-Century Italian Culture" in *Strumenti critici/n.s.*, a. I, (settembre 1986), 343-376.

²Primo Levi, *I sommersi e i salvati* (Turin: Einaudi, 1986), 21; Risa Sodi, "An Interview with Primo Levi," *Partisan Review LIV*, (Summer 1987): 363.

³Levi, *La ricerca delle radici* (Turin: Einaudi, 1981), x.

⁴Levi, *I sommersi e i salvati*, 11.

Chapter I: *AL DI QUA DEL BENE E DEL MALE*: JUSTICE IN DANTE'S *INFERNO* AND IN PRIMO LEVI'S FIRST AND LAST BOOKS

¹Philippe Delhaye, "Giustizia," in *Enciclopedia dantesca* (Rome: Istituto della enciclopedia italiana, 1971), 233.

²See *I sommersi e i salvati*, chapters 1 and 5.

³Primo Levi, *I sommersi e i salvati*, 14 (the original, of which my quote is a paraphrase, reads, "...i due sono nella stessa trappola, ma è l'oppressore, e solo lui, che l'ha approntata e che l'ha fatta scattare, e se ne soffre, è giusto che ne soffra.")

⁴Deut., 6:4-7.

⁵The biblical Sh'ma concludes with the verses, "And you shall bind them as a sign upon your hand, and they shall be as frontlets between your eyes. And you shall write them on the doorposts of your house and upon your gates." (Deut., 6:8-9). Later in the same chapter, God's jealousy and divine wrath are manifested through his warning against the sin of idolatry: "You shall not go after other gods, of the gods of the people who are round about you; for the Lord your God in the midst of you is a jealous God; lest the anger of the Lord your God be kindled against you and he destroy you from off the face of the earth." (Deut., 6:14-15). While this threat is substantially more terrifying than the tamer conclusion of Levi's *Shema*, it also addresses a substantially different set of propositions.

⁶For a description camp conditions at Fossoli, first under the Italian Fascist militia and then under the German SS, see my interview with Levi, "A Last Interview with Primo Levi," in *Present Tense* (May/June 1988).

⁷Levi, *Se questo è un uomo* (Turin: Einaudi, 1958), 11-12.

⁸Levi, La ricerca delle radici, xi.

⁹It is interesting to note that Levi begins *La ricerca delle radici* (a collection of the works that most influenced him), with the book of Job and the theme of justice—even though justice is not explicitly mentioned in the list quoted above. He calls this particular selection "Il giusto oppresso dall'ingiustizia":

> Perché incominciare dal Giobbe? Perché questa storia splendida e atroce racchiude in sé le domande di tutti i tempi, quelle a cui l'uomo non ha trovato risposta finora, né la troverà mai, ma la cercherà sempre perché ne ha bisogno per vivere, per capire se stesso e il mondo. Giobbe è il giusto oppresso dall'ingiustizia. È vittima di una crudele scommessa fra Satana e Dio: che farà Giobbe, pio, sano, ricco e felice, se sarà toccato negli averi, e poi negli affetti familiari, e poi sulla stessa sua pelle? Ebbene, Giobbe il giusto, degradato ad animale da esperimento, si comporta come farebbe ognuno di noi: dapprima china il capo e loda Dio ("Accetteremmo da Dio il bene e non il male?"), poi le sue difese crollano. Povero, orbato dei figli, coperto di piaghe, siede tra i rifiuti grattandosi con un coccio, e contende con Dio. È una contesa disuguale: Dio creatore di meraviglie e di mostri lo schiaccia sotto la sua onnipotenza. (Levi, *La ricerca delle radici*, 5)

[10] In Italy, beginning at least as early as 1938, Jews were considered a race, not a religious group; more to the point, they were considered a separate race from the Italians (whom, Fascist racialist "experts" defined as Aryans).

[11] Levi, *I sommersi e i salvati*, 18.

[12] James Sterba, *The Demands of Justice* (Notre Dame, Ind.: Notre Dame University Press, 1980), 76.

[13] See Thomas Keneally, *Schindler's List* (New York: Simon & Schuster, 1982), the story of how Austrian industrialist Oscar Schindler managed to save hundreds of Jews from the Lodz ghetto. Several of the Nazi guards in charge of overseeing the prisoners in the various camps described in that book expressed a desire to request transfer to the Eastern front in order to expiate their actions in the camps; only one or two of those mentioned in the book actually followed through on those thoughts.

[14] Levi, *I sommersi e i salvati*, 166-167.

[15] Morris Ginsberg, *On Justice in Society* (Ithaca, N.Y.: Cornell University Press, 1965), 67.

[16] Levi explains that the "usefulness" of this violence is allegorized in *Gulliver's Travels*, in which the Struldbruggs inhabit an immortal, and therefore unlivable world, one which is far more "violent" that our own. Similarly, Daniel Callahan, a medical ethicist, makes an interesting case for the "violence" of unnaturally prolonged life in his latest book, *Setting Limits* (New York: Simon & Schuster, 1987).

[17] Actually, the character was Fra Alberigo (*Inferno* XXXIII, 109).

[18] "E io non lil' apersi/e cortesia fu lui esser villano," (*Inferno* XXXIII, 149-50; English translation by Thomas William Parsons).

[19] Sodi, *Partisan Review* 3: 362-363.

[20] Levi, *I sommersi e i salvati*, 85.

[21] Guido Lopez, "Se non lui, chi?," *Shalom* 4 (aprile 1987): 23.

[22] Alan H. Gilbert, *Dante's Conception of Justice* (New York: AMS Press, Inc., 1965), v.

[23] Dante Alighieri, *The Divine Comedy*, trans. and ed., Charles S. Singleton (Princeton, N.J.: Princeton University Press, 1970), Vol. I, *Inferno* III, 4.

[24] Delhaye, *Enciclopedia dantesca*, 234.

[25] *Ibid*, 235.

[26] *Virtus morales est habitus electivus*, Thomas Aquinas, *Commentary*; quoted in Gilbert, *Dante's Conception of Justice*, 31.

[27] Gilbert, *Dante's Conception of Justice*, 50.
[28] Levi, *I sommersi e i salvati*, 18.
[29] Levi, *Se questo è un uomo*, 107-108.
[30] Levi, *I sommersi e i salvati*, 111.
[31] Morton Kaplan, *Justice, Human Nature and Political Obligation* (New York: The Free Press, 1976), vii.
[32] Sodi, *Partisan Review* 3, 364.
[33] Levi, *I sommersi e i salvati*, 31.
[34] Sterba, *The Demands of Justice*, 64.
[35] See Chapter III on the memory of offense.
[36] Sterba, *The Demands of Justice*, 64.
[37] Kaplan, *Justice, Human Nature and Political Obligation*, vii; Sterba, *The Demands of Justice*, 67.
[38] Dante, *Inferno* XVIII, 95.
[39] Sodi, *Partisan Review* 3, 364.
[40] Morris Ginsberg, *On Justice in Society* (Ithaca, N.Y.: Cornell University Press, 1965), 62.
[41] Gilbert, *Dante's Conception of Justice*, vi.
[42] Herbert G. May and Bruce M. Metzger, *Oxford Annotated Bible with Apocrypha* (New York: Oxford University Press, 1965), 94 (note to Exodus 21:22-25).
[43] Gilbert, *Dante's Conception of Justice*, 3.
[44] Anthony Cassell, *Dante's Fearful Art of Justice* (Toronto: University of Toronto Press, 1984), 4; Gilbert, *Dante's Conception of Justice*, vi.
[45] Dante encounters these characters as he descends the circles of the inferno: Farinata (4th circle), Pier della Vigna (2nd round of the 7th circle), Brunetto Latini (3rd round of the 7th circle) and Master Adam (10th bolgia of the 8th circle).
[46] John Freccero, *Dante, The Poetics of Conversion* (Cambridge: Harvard University Press, 1986), 105.
[47] *Ibid*, 105.
[48] To give but a few examples: Rudolf Höss, commandant at Auschwitz, was executed on a hill overlooking Auschwitz in 1947; Franz Stangl, commandant at Treblinka, was sentenced to life imprisonment in Germany in 1971 and died in the same year; Rudolf Hess, the Reich minister for party affairs, died in Spandau prison in Berlin on August 17, 1987; Klaus Barbie, the Gestapo chief of Lyons, was sentenced to life imprisonment in France on July 6, 1987; John Demjanjuk was convicted of war

crimes, crimes against the Jewish people, crimes against humanity, and crimes against a persecuted people by an Israeli court on April 18, 1988; and Kurt Waldheim (the president of Austria) and Werner von Braun (former deputy administrator of NASA) have both been accused, though never tried or convicted, of war crimes (see "Removing the Welcome Mat: The U.S. Bars Waldheim," *Time*, 11 May 1987; and "Da Dachau alla luna," *L'Espresso*, 2 agosto 1987).

[49] Jacobellis v. Ohio, 378 U.S. 184 at 197 (1964).

[50] Jean Améry, né Hans Meyer, was an Austrian philologist and philosopher, and a thoroughly assimilated Jew. He was tortured by the Gestapo for belonging to the Belgian resistance and then deported to Auschwitz as a Jew, where for a time, Améry and Levi were confined to the same barracks. In 1978, Améry committed suicide. "The Intellectual at Auschwitz," a chapter of *I sommersi e i salvati*, considers Améry's story in more detail.

[51] Sodi, *Partisan Review* 3, 363-364.

[52] Levi, *I sommersi e i salvati*, 110.

[53] Along these lines, it is interesting to consider that, in the *Inferno*, it is entirely possible that Dante did all the sinners (or at least the Christian-era sinners) therein a grave injustice by condemning them at all. According to medieval Christian doctrine, a person who repents, even on his deathbed, is totally absolved of all past sins, no matter how heinous or reprehensible. Who is to say, Dante included, that Brunetto Latini or Guido Cavalcante or Conte Ugolino did not repent their sins with their last breaths! Nonetheless (and the fact that he describes real people notwithstanding), we must still allow Dante his fictive universe and the liberty to interpret as he choses the events he inserts in his poem; that is, after all, part of our reader's "contract" with him. However, we might point out that Dante did allow at least one such instance of deathbed repentence in the *Commedia*: Manfredo in Canto III of *Purgatory*.

Boccaccio, Dante's sybaritic contemporary, refused to pass this sort of Dantean "God's-eye judgment" in his story of Ser Ciappelletto, who "con una falsa confessione inganna uno santo frate, e muorsi; et essendo stato un pessimo uomo in vita, in morte è reputato per Sante, e chiamato san Ciappelletto" (Giovanni Boccaccio, *Il decamerone* [Milan: Hoepli, 1932], 22). Boccaccio ends his story with this humorous monition:

> Così adunque visse e morì ser Cepperello da Prato, e santo divenne come avete udito. Il quale negar non voglio esser

possibile, lui essere beato nella presenza di Dio, per ciò che, come che la sua vita fosse scelerata e malvagia, egli poté in su l'estremo aver sì fatta contrizione, che per avventura Iddio ebbe misericordia di lui, e nel suo regno il ricevette. Ma per ciò che questo n'è occulto, secondo quello che ne può apparire ragiono, e dico, costui più tosto dovere essere nelle mani del diavolo in perdizione, che in paradiso.

[54] Sodi, *Partisan Review* 3, 364.
[55] Levi, *Se questo è un uomo*, 13.
[56] Dante, *Inferno* III, 25-27.

Chapter II: NEITHER *IN BONO* NOR *IN MALO*: THE GREY ZONE AND THE NEUTRAL SINNERS

[1] Levi, *I sommersi e i salvati*, 25.
[2] *Ibid*, 25.
[3] Since first used by David Rousset in *L'univers concentrationnaire* (Paris: Editions du Pavois, 1946), this phrase has been oft-repeated in Holocaust literature (by Primo Levi as well). One of the most startling uses of it outside Holocaust literature comes from Umberto Eco in his *Postille a Il nome della rosa* (Milan: Bompiani, 1984): in explaining why he set his scholarly murder-mystery in a Benedictine abbey, Eco writes on page 20, "Avevo molti problemi. Volevo un luogo chiuso, un universo concentrazionario..." One cannot help but feel Eco inserted this phrase primarily to jolt his reader.
[4] Levi, *I sommersi e i salvati*, 27.
[5] Freccero, *Dante, The Poetics of Conversion*, 96.
[6] Dante, *Inferno* III 31.
[7] Freccero, *Dante, The Poetics of Conversion*, 117.
[8] Dante Alighieri, *The Divine Comedy*, Italian text with English translation and commentary by John D. Sinclair (New York: Oxford University Press, 1979), 54.
[9] The last line of Dante's closely resembles a verse from Job 14:22: "He feels only the pain of his own body, and he mourns only for himself."

Interestingly enough, these lines were included in the selection from Job which Levi uses to open *La ricerca delle radici*; the similarity between Job and Dante is even more striking in the Italian version: "E la sua carne *per sé* si tortura, E la sua anima *per sé* si dispera." [italics mine]

[10] Freccero, *Dante, The Poetics of Conversion*, 111-112.

[11] Dante, *The Divine Comedy* (1979), 54-55.

[12] Freccero, *Dante, The Poetics of Conversion*, 114.

[13] *Ibid*, 114.

[14] *Ibid*, 116.

[15] Levi dedicates seven pages of his chapter on the grey zone in *I sommersi e i salvati* to the Rumkowski story, the story of the president of the Lodz Judenrat during the Nazi occupation. While a Nazi collaborator and accomplice, Rumkowski also saw himself as a "Messiah, a savior of his people":

> Paradossalmente, alla sua identificazione con gli oppressori si alterna o si affianca un'identificazione con gli oppressi poiché l'uomo, dice Thomas Mann, è una creatura confusa; e tanto più confusa diventa, possiamo aggiungere, quanto più è sottoposta a tensioni: allora sfugge al nostro giudizio, così come impazzisce una bussola al polo magnetico."(Levi, *I sommersi e i salvati*, 48).

Levi also writes that Rumkowski's story encompasses the entire thematics of the grey zone; it poses more questions than it answers; and it cries out to be understood. For a more detailed analysis of Chaim Rumkowski, see Lucjan Dobroszycki, ed., *The Chronicle of the Lodz Ghetto, 1941-1944* (New Haven, Conn.: Yale University Press, 1984).

[16] Levi, *I sommersi e i salvati*, 45.

[17] *Ibid*, 44.

[18] Levi, *I sommersi e i salvati*, 44.

[19] Levi, *I sommersi e i salvati* 45; the phrase "death of the soul," as quoted by Levi, comes from Paul Vercors, *Les armes de la nuit* (Paris: Albin Michel, 1953).

[20] Levi, *I sommersi e i salvati*, 15.

[21] *Ibid*, 130.

[22] Levi, *I sommersi e i salvati*, 39. Levi tells the story of a survivor of the last squad at Auschwitz, Miklos Nyiszli, in the chapter on the grey zone in *I sommersi e i salvati*. Other accounts can be had from personal

memoirs and from the film *Shoah* (1985), which tells the story of ex-Special Squad member Filip Mueller. When I spoke to Levi in June 1986, *Shoah* had not been released in Italy. He was very interested in hearing my account of it, marvelling that it had been shown six times during the course of the 1986 Holocaust Memorial Week at the University of Massachusetts at Amherst [where I was a student at the time].

[23] *Ibid*, 42.
[24] *Ibid*, 43.
[25] *Ibid*, 45.
[26] *Ibid*, 34; Sodi, *Partisan Review* 3, 358.
[27] Levi, *I sommersi e i salvati*, 34.
[28] *Ibid*, 34-35.
[29] Sodi, *Partisan Review* 3, 365.
[30] *Ibid*, 365-366. The issue of "fabricating a set of truths" will become important in the next chapter, when we discuss the "memory of offense."
[31] Levi, *I sommersi e i salvati*, 106; Levi, *Se questo è un uomo*, 153-154.
[32] Levi, *Se questo è un uomo*, 153.
[33] *Ibid*, 70-71.
[34] *Ibid*, 50.
[35] *Ibid*, 113.
[36] See "Il ritorno di Lorenzo" in *Lilìt e altri racconti* (Turin: Einaudi, 1981). After Levi's return to Italy in 1945, he paid Lorenzo a visit at his home:

> Trovai un uomo stanco; non stanco del cammino, stanco mortalmente, di una stanchezza senza ritorno. Andammo a bere insieme all'osteria, e dalle poche parole che riuscii a strappargli compresi che il suo margine di amore per la vita si era assottigliato, era quasi scomparso...Il mondo lo aveva visto, non gli piaceva, lo sentiva andare in rovina; vivere non gli interessava più.

Lorenzo died a short time later. Levi comments, "Lui, che non era una reduce, era morto del male dei reduci."

[37] Levi, *Se questo è un uomo*, 187-188.
[38] Dante, *Inferno* III, 126.
[39] Dante, *Inferno* XII, 37; See John Singleton's comments on *i tristi* in

The Divine Comedy: Vol. 2, *Inferno*, (Princeton, N.J.: Princeton University Press, 1970), 118-119.

[40]Dante, *Inferno* XXIII, 37.

[41]Not all commentators agree with this analysis. John Freccero states in Alighieri, *op. cit.*, 45:

> [The neutral angels] simply did not act [as did those who rebelled with Satan], but remained frozen in a state of aversion from God. It is pointless to ask whether they were better or worse than the lowest of sinners, for they do not fit into any category, after the initial division of heavenly light from infernal dark...To be deprived of action is to be deprived of love, and love is the law of Dante's cosmos, determining all classifications. There remains nothing for them but the vaguely defined vestibule of hell, and they merit no more than a glance from the pilgrim before he passes on to the realm of love perverted.

[42]Dante, *Inferno* III, 50.

Chapter III: OBLIVISCENCE AND REMINISCENCE: MEMORY AND THE MEMORY OF OFFENSE

[1]See Philip Boswood Ballard, *Obliviscence and Reminiscence* (Cambridge: Cambridge University Press, 1913).

[2]Levi, *I sommersi e i salvati*, 13.

[3]Stanley Munsat, *The Concept of Memory* (New York: Random House, 1967), 12.

[4]*Ibid*, 12.

[5]Levi, *I sommersi e i salvati*, 14.

[6]Munsat, *The Concept of Memory*, xiv.

[7]See Gita Serenyi, *Into That Darkness: The Journey from Mercy Killing to Mass Murder* (London: Deutsch, 1974) and Rudolf Höss, *Kommandant in Auschwitz* (Stuttgart: Deutsche Verlags-Anstalt, 1958).

[8]Levi, *I sommersi e i salvati*, 17.

[9] *Ibid*, 14.

[10] *Ibid*, back cover (paperback edition).

[11] *Ibid*, 16.

[12] Sodi, *Partisan Review* 3, 358.

[13] Sigmund Freud, "The Ego and the Id and Other Works," in *The Standard Edition of the Complete Psychological Works of Sigmund Freud*, trans. James Strachey et. al. London: Hogarth Press and The Institute of Psychoanalysis, 1953-1974, Vol. XIX [1923-1925], 236-237.

[14] Levi, *I sommersi e i salvati*, 19.

[15] Levi, *Se questo è un uomo*, 42.

[16] *Ibid*, 43.

[17] "Selections" were common in the Auschwitz camp system, beginning as early as July 4, 1942. They were used to thin out the camp population, bloated, especially after the fall of 1943, by new freightloads of Eastern European Jews. Elie Wiesel's book *Night* deals dramatically with the ruthless selection of October 1944.

[18] Levi, *I sommersi e i salvati*, 14.

[19] It is also interesting at this juncture to compare one assessment of Primo Levi made after his death as "il custode della memoria" (Tullia Zevi, *Il Giornale*, April 12, 1987) with Levi's own self-definition as "the bearer of the secret." While the first comment is eulogistic and faintly totemistic, Levi's own self-appraisal contains both the elements of memory and knowledge: to bear a secret is to be possessed by an irrepressible state of knowing. See also Levi, *I sommersi e i salvati*, 6.

[20] Delhaye, *Enciclopedia dantesca*, 888-889.

[21] Glauco Cambon, *Dante's Craft: Studies in Language and Style* (Minneapolis: University of Minnesota Press, 1969), 70; see also Chapter IV on the "noble sinners" in general.

[22] Dante, *The Divine Comedy* (1979), 331.

[23] Comment by George Santayana, quoted in Dante, *The Divine Comedy* (1979), 83.

[24] *Ibid*, 331.

[25] Freccero, *Dante, The Poetics of Conversion*, 15.

[26] Dante, *Inferno* XXV, 119.

[27] Cassell, *Dante's Fearful Art of Justice*, 86.

[28] Freccero, *Dante, The Poetics of Conversion*, 7.

[29] Levi, *Se questo è un uomo*, 42.

[30] *Ibid*, 142.

[31] Dante, *Inferno* XXVI, 119-120.
[32] Levi, *Se questo è un uomo*, 144.
[33] *Ibid*, 145.
[34] Cassell, *Dante's Fearful Art of Justice*, 86.
[35] Levi, *I sommersi e i salvati*, 21.
[36] Dante, *Inferno* XXVII, 57.
[37] See note 48, Chapter II, for the current status of Barbie, Demjanjuk and Linnas.
[38] *Time*, 11 May 1987.
[39] Quoted in: Alfonso Maieru, "Memoria," in *Enciclopedia dantesca* (Rome: Istituto della enciclopedia italiana, 1971), 888.
[40] *Ibid*, 888; Dante, *Purgatorio* XXV, 83-88.
[41] Dante, *The Divine Comedy*: Vol. 2, *Purgatory*, 820.
[42] Dante, *Purgatorio* XXVIII, 130.
[43] Dante, *The Divine Comedy*: Vol. 2, *Purgatory*, 687; Maieru, *Enciclopedia dantesca*, 629-630.
[44] Dante, *Inferno* XXXIII, 138.
[45] Herbert G. May and Bruce M. Metzger, *Oxford Annotated Bible with Apocrypha*, Psalms 137:1.
[46] Levi, *Terza Pagina: Saggi e racconti di Primo Levi* (Turin: La Stampa, 1987).

CONCLUSION

[1] "Non si è suicidato," *Panorama*, 3 maggio 1987, 62-63.
[2] *Ibid*, 63.
[3] Mario Rigoni Stern in "Primo Levi: La memoria del dolore," *La Nazione* (Florence, Italy), 12 aprile 87, 3.
[4] Ben Sargent, *The Austin-American Statesman*, reprinted in *The New York Times*, 31 May 1987, Week in Review sec., 5
[5] Levi, *I sommersi e i salvati*, 13-14.
[6] See "Russian Nationalists Test Gorbachev," *The New York Times*, 23 May 1987, 2; and "For Soviet Jews, Emigration Poses a Divisive Issue," *The New York Times*, 6 December 1987, 2.

[7]Giorgio Bassani, *Il giardino dei Finzi-Contini* (Turin: Einaudi, 1962), 224.

[8]Giorgio Bassani, "Una lapide in Via Mazzini," in *Dentro le mura* (Milan: Mondadori, 1973).

[9]Sodi, *Partisan Review* 3, 355-356.

[10]Levi, *I sommersi e i salvati*, 56; see also Dante, *Inferno* I, 22-27

> E come quei che con lena affannata,
>   uscito fuor dal pelago a la riva,
>   si volge a *l'acqua perigliosa* e guata,
>   così l'animo mio, ch'ancor fuggiva,
>   si volse a retro a rimirar lo passo.
> [italics mine]

BIBLIOGRAPHY

Selected Works by Levi

Levi, Primo, *Lilìt e altri racconti*. Turin: Einaudi, 1981.
—. *L'osteria di Brema*. Milan: Scheiwiller, 1975.
—. *La ricerca delle radici*. Turin: Einaudi, 1981.
—. *Se questo è un uomo*. Turin: Einaudi, 1965.
—. *I sommersi e i salvati*. Turin: Einaudi, 1986.
—. *Terza Pagina: Racconti e saggi di Primo Levi*. Turin: La Stampa, 1987.
—. "The Memory of Offense" in Hartman,Geoffrey H., ed., *Bitberg in Moral and Political Perspective*. Bloomington, Ind.: Indiana University Press, 1986, 130-137.
—. *La tregua*. Turin: Einaudi, 1963.

A Brief Levi Bibliography

Atlas, James. "The Survivor's Suicide." *Vanity Fair*, 51 (January 1988).
Cicioni, Mirna. "Bridges of Knowledge: Rereading Primo Levi." *Spunti e ricerche*, vol. 3, 1987.
Grassano. Giuseppe. *Primo Levi*. Florence: La Nuova Italia, 1981
Greer, Germaine. "Germaine Greer Talks to Primo Levi." *The Literary Review*, November 1985.
James, Clive. "Last Will and Testament." *The New Yorker*, May 23, 1988.
Lopez, Guido. "Se non lui, chi.". *Shalom*, n. 4, Aprile 1987.

Risk, Mirna. "Razionalità e coscienza etica di Primo Levi." *Italian Studies*, Vol. XXXIV, 1979.

Segrè, Giorgio. "Intervista a Primo Levi." *Ha-Tikvà*, Anno XXXI, N. 307 Marzo-Aprile 1979.

Sodi, Risa. "An Interview with Primo Levi." *Partisan Review* LIV (Summer 1987)

–. "A Last Talk with Primo Levi". *Present Tense*, May/June 1988. Reprinted in *Jewish Profiles: The Best of Present Tense*. New York: Jacob Aronson, Inc. (forthcoming).

Stille, Alexander. "Primo Levi: Reconciling the Man and the Writer." *New York Times Book Review*, May 5, 1987.

"*I sommersi e i salvati*: Intervista a Primo Levi, dopo l'uscita del suo ultimo libro." *Bolletino della Communità Israelitica di Milano*, Anno LXII, n. 7, Luglio 1986.

Vincenti, Fiora. *Invito alla lettura di Primo Levi*. Turin: Mursia, 1973.

Dante and His Contemporaries

Alighieri, Dante. *The Divine Comedy* (Italian text with English translation and commentary by John D. Sinclair). New York: Oxford University Press, 1979.

Alighieri, Dante. *The Divine Comedy* (Italian text with English translation and commentary by Charles S. Singleton). Princeton: Princeton University Press, 1973.

Baranski, Zygmunt G. "The Power of Influence: Aspects of Dante's Presence in Twentieth-Century Italian Culture." *Strumenti critici*/n.s., a. I, n. 3 (settembre 1986), 343-376.

Boccaccio, Giovanni. *Il decamerone*. Milan: Hoepli, 1932.

Cambon, Clauco. *Dante's Craft: Studies in Language and Style*. Minneopolis: University of Minnesota Press, 1969.

Delhaye, Philippe. "Giustizia," in *Enciclopedia dantesca*. Rome: Istituto della enciclopedia italiana, 1971, 223-235.

Freccero, John. *Dante, The Poetics of Conversion*. Cambridge: Harvard University Press, 1986.

Mazzamuto, Pietro. "Lete," in *Enciclopedia dantesca*. Rome: Istituto della enciclopedia italiana, 1971, 629-630.

Mazzotta, Giuseppe. *Dante, Poet of the Desert*. Princeton, NJ: Princeton University Press, 1979.

Jews in Italy

Arieti, Silvano. *The Parnas*. New York: Basic Books, 1979.
Bassani, Giorgio. *Dentro le mura*. Milan: Mondadori, 1973.
—. *Il giardino dei Finzi-Contini*. Turin: Einaudi, 1962.
Levi-Montalcini, Rita. *In Praise of Imperfection*. New York: Sloan Foundation Science Series/Basic Books, 1989.
Mann, Vivian B., ed. *Gardens and Ghettos: The Art of Jewish Life in Italy*. Berkeley: University of California Press, 1989. Includes Preface by Primo Levi.
Milano, Attilio. *Storia degli ebrei in Italia*. Turin: Einaudi, 1963.
Jesurum, Stefano. *Essere ebrei in Italia*. Milan: Longanesi & C., 1987.
Segre, Augusto. *Memorie di vita ebraica: Casale Monferrato-Rome-Gerusalemme, 1918-1960*. Rome: Bonacci, 1979.
Segre, Vittorio. *Storia di un ebreo fortunato*. Milan: Bompiani, 1985.

Justice

Callahan, Daniel. *Setting Limits*. New York: Simon & Schuster, 1987.
Cassell, Anthony K. *Dante's Fearful Art of Justice*. Toronto: University of Toronto Press, 1984
Croce, Benedetto. *Libertà e giustizia*. Bari, Italy: Giuseppe Laterza e figli, 1944.
Daniels, Norman. *Reading Rawls: Critical Studies on Rawls' Theory of Justice*. New York: Basic Books.
Gilbert, Alan H. *Dante's Conception of Justice*. New York: AMS Press, Inc., 1965.
Ginsberg, Morris. *On Justice in Society*. Ithaca, NY: Cornell University Press, 1965.

Kaplan, Morton. *Justice, Human Nature and Political Obligation.* New York: The Free Press, 1976.

Sterba, James. *The Demands of Justice.* Notre Dame, Ind.: Notre Dame University Press, 1980.

Memory

Ballard, Philip Boswood. *Obliviscence and Reminiscence.* Cambridge: Cambridge University Press, 1913.

Johnson, George. "Memory: Learning How It Works." *New York Times Magazine*, Aug. 9, 1987, 16-21, 33-35, 57.

Loftus, Elizabeth. "Trials of an Expert Witness: Research Into Memory Shows that People Often Remember Things Differently from the Way They Were." *Newsweek*, vol. 109, June 29, 1987.

Loftus, Gregory R. and Loftus, Elizabeth F. *Human Memory: The Processing of Information.* Hillsdale, NJ: Lawrence Erdlaum Assoc., 1975.

Maieru, Alfonso. "Memoria," in *Enciclopedia dantesca*. Rome: Istituto della enciclopedia italiana, 1971, 888-892.

Munsat, Stanley. *The Concept of Memory.* New York: Random House, 1967.

Roskies, David G. "Memory," in Cohen, Arthur A. and Mendes-Flohr, Paul, ed., *Contemporary Jewish Religious Thought.* New York: Charles Scriber's Sons, 1987.

Holocaust and Jewish Concerns

Bower, Tom. "Da Dachau alla luna." *L'Espresso*, 2 agosto 1987, 82-89.

De Felice, Renzo. *Storia degli ebrei italiani sotto il fascismo*, 3rd ed. Turin: Einaudi, 1972.

Michaelis, Meir. *Mussolini and the Jews.* Oxford: The Clarendon Press, 1978.

Dobroszycki, Lucjan, ed. *The Chronicle of the Lodz Ghetto, 1941-44.* New Haven: Yale University Press, 1984.

Höss, Rudolf. *Kommandant in Auschwitz.* Stuttgart: Deutsche Verlags-Ansalt, 1958.

Howe, Irving. "Writing and the Holocaust: How Literature Has, and Has Not, Met Its Greatest Challenge." *New Republic* 195 (27 October 1986), pp. 27-39.

Keneally, Thomas. *Schindler's List.* New York: Simon & Schuster, 1982.

Rousset, David. *Univers concentrationnaire.* Paris: Editions du Pavois, 1946.

Roskies, David. G. *Against the Apocalypse.* Cambridge: Harvard University Press, 1984.

Sereny, Gitta. *Into That Darkness: The Journey from Mercy Killing to Mass Murder.* London: Deutsch, 1974.

Wiesel, Elie. *Night.* New York: Avon Books, 1969.

Young, James. "The Texture of Memory: Holocaust Memorials and Meaning", *Holocaust and Genocide Studies,* vol. 4, no. 1, 1989.

Zuccotti, Susan. *The Italians and the Holocaust.* New York: Basic Books, 1986.

Other Works of Interest

Buttrick, George Arthur, Commentary Editor. *The Interpreter's Bible.* New York: Abdington Press, 1955.

Eco, Umberto. *Postille a Il nome della rosa.* Milan: Bompiani, 1984.

Fay, Edward Allen. *Concordance of the Divine Comedy.* Graz, Austria: Akademische Druck - U. Verlagsanstalt, 1966 [orig. 1888].

Freud, Sigmund. "The Ego and the Id and Other Works," in *The Standard Edition of the Complete Psychological Works of Sigmund Freud,* trans. James Strachey et. al. London: Hogarth Press and The Institute of Psychoanalysis, 1953-1974, Vol. XIX [1923-1925], 236-237.

May, Herbert G. and Metzger, Bruce M. *Oxford Annotated Bible with Apocrypha.* New York: Oxford University Press, 1965.

INDEX

Aeneid, 77
Acheron (river), 44
"Alberto," 41-42, 58-59, *See* Grey Zone
Argenti, Filippo, 61
Alberigo, Fra, 2
Améry, Jean, 25, 54
Amor Proprio, 33, 74, *See* Natural Love of Self
Aquinas, Thomas, 9, 17
Argenti, Filippo, 61
Aristotle, 17, 29, 60
Auschwitz, 2, 5, 7, 9, 27, 32, 37, 42, 47, 53, 58, 67, 69, 78, 87, 89, *See* Höss, Rudolph
Averroës, 60
Avicenna, 60
Ballard, Phillip Boswood, 49
Barbie, Klaus, 74, 83
Bassani, Giorgio, 85-87
   Il giardino dei Finzi-Contini, 85
   "Una lapide in Via Mazzini," 86
Befehlnotstand, 35, 36, 38, 46, *See* Constraint
Birkenau, 37, 43, 58
Bocca degli Abbati, 13
Buchenwald, 87
Buna, 19, 36
Caccianemico, Vendico, 63

Cambon, Glauco, 62
Cassell, Anthony, 70
Cavalcanti, Guido, 62, 65
Cavani, Liliana, 38-39
   The Night Porter, 38-39
"Charles," 43, *See* Grey Zone
Coleridge, Samuel Taylor, 87-88
   The Rime of the Ancient Mariner," 87-88
Constantine the African, 60
Constraint, 39-40, 46
Contrapasso, 22, 23-24, 29, 51, 62, 64, 70, 72, 73, *See* Retribution, *See also Lex talionis*
Dante, 1, 2, 5, 8, 14-15, 17, 18, 20, 21-22, 24, 29, 32-34, 44, 45, 50-51, 60-67, 68, 70-73, 76-78, 89
   Convivio, 15, 76
   De Monarchia, 15
   Divine Comedy, 1, 5, 13, 15, 21-22, 50, 62, 64, 76
   Ninth Epistle, 15
de Born, Bertran, 64, 73
De Cori, Ferruccio, 3
Delhaye, Phillip, 15
della Vigna, Pier, 23, 24, 33, 45, 47, 62, 64, 65
Demjanjuk, John, 57, 59, 74, 83, *See* Treblinka

Deuteronomy, 7, 49
Dis, 46
Dostoyevski, Feodor, 39, 84
  Brothers Karamazov, 27
  Crime and Punishment, 13
Elias, 19, 24-25, *See* Justice
Epstein, Pinchas, 57
Eunoé, 55, 77-78
Exodus, 23
Farinata, 23, 24, 62
Final Solution, 6, 11
Forgiveness, 20-21, 25, 27-28, *See* Pardon
Fossoli (internment camp), 9
Freccero, John, 24, 32, 33, 34, 65, 66
  The Poetics of Conversion, 32
Freud, Sigmund, 56, 85
  Die Verneinung, 56
Galenus, 60
Genesis, 77
Gilbert, Alan, 22, 29
Ginsberg, Morris, 8, 22
  On Justice in Society, 8
Grey Zone, 2, 5-6, 31-32, 34, 35, 36, 38, 39-41, 45, 47, 53, 75, 89
Griffolino da Arezzo, 73, 74
Guido da Montefeltro, 71, 73
Habitus, 17, 70
Hart, H. L. A., 12
Hitler, Adolf, 12
Holocaust, 3, 8, 11, 34, 42, 52-53, 74, 79, 83-84, 85, 89
Höss, Rudolph, 27, 53, 54, 59, *See* Auschwitz
Inferno, 1, 2, 14, 15-16, 18, 20, 22, 23, 26, 28, 44, 46, 51, 60, 61, 63, 66, 70, 72; Canto I, 32, 61, 66; II, 32, 61; III, 17, 32, 33, 45, 46, 62; V, 45; VII, 15-16, 44, 45; XII, 15-16; XIII, 45, 63; XIX, 71; XX, 44; XXVI, 65, 68; XXVII, 68, 71, 73; XXIX, 15-16, 73; XXX, 71, 73; XXXIII, 62, 70; XXXIV, 77
Isidore of Seville, 60
Jason, 21
Justice, 2, 3, 5, 8, 10, 15, 16-17, 18, 19-20, 23-29, 38, 43, 49, 59-60, 79, 83-84, 89; divine justice in Dante, 15-17, 18, 20, 72; divine justice in Levi, 21; commutative, 8; corrective, 8; distributive, 8; relativism and, 21; utilitarianism and, 21, *See* Retribution; *See also* Legal Systems
Kaplan, Milton, 20
Latini, Brunetto, 23, 27, 62
Legal Systems, 11, 18, 19-20, 21
Lethe, 55, 77-78
Lex Talionis, 23, 26; *See Contrapasso*
Levi, Primo, 1, 2, 5, 7-10, 11, 13, 15, 18, 19-21, 22, 24-27, 29, 31, 34, 36, 38, 39-43, 44-47, 51, 52, 53-54, 55, 56, 57-60, 62, 63, 66, 67-69, 70, 71, 75, 78-79, 81-85, 86, 87, 89
"Il disgelo," 79
L'osteria di Brema, 7
La ricerca delle radici, 10
Se questo è un uomo, 1, 2, 6, 9, 19, 27, 35, 41, 43, 45, 50, 51, 57, 58, 67-69, 78, 87
"Shema," 6-7, 8, 27
I sommersi e i salvati, 1, 2, 13, 14,

18, 19, 21, 25, 31, 40, 41, 45, 49, 55, 58, 78, 82, 85, 87
Levi-Montalcini, Rita, 81-82
Leviticus, 23
Linnas, Karl, 74, 83, *See* Tartu
"Lorenzo," 43, *See* Grey Zone
Master Adam, 23, 73
Memory, 2, 49, 51-57, 60-63, 64, 65, 66, 67-69, 70-72, 73, 74-75, 76-77, 78, 79, 83, 84-86, 89, *See* Memory of Offense, *See also* Remembering
Memory of Offense, 2, 9, 49, 51, 57-58, 59, 70, 72, 77, 79
Mens Rea, 12, 28
Moro, Aldo, 13
Muhsfeld, SS Commander, 37-38
Munsat, Stanley, 52, 54, 61
   The Concept of Memory, 52
Natural Love of Self, 26, 33, 34, 46, *See Amor Proprio*
Nazis, 2, 6, 11, 12, 13, 14, 18, 36, 37, 40, 63, 66, 74, 75, 85
Neutral Sinners, 2, 9, 31, 32, 36, 45-46
Pamyat, 84-85
Paradise, 22
Pardon, 25-26, 28
Pellepoix, Darquier de, 53-54
Plato
  Menon, 60
Platinus, 60
Plotinus, 66
Psalm 137, 78
Pope Boniface, 18, 71
Pope Nicholas III, 18, 71
Protocols of the Elders of Zion, 85

Punishment, 8, 11, 21, 22, 23, 24, 26, 27, 28, 46, 51, 52
Purgatory, 22, 26, 55; Canto XXV, 72; XXXIII, 77
Red Brigades, 13
Remembering, 52, 53, 72, 76
Retribution, 8, 19, 21, 22, 23, 63, *See* Contrapasso, *See also Lex Talionis*
Revenge, 21-23, 24-26, 28
Rigoni-Stern, Mario, 82
Rosenberg, Eliyahu, 57
Rumkowski, Chaim, 34, *See* Grey Zone
Sade, Marquis de, 39
St. Ambrose, 66
St. Augustine, 60, 72
Schadenfreude, 14, 26, 28
Sh'ma, 7, 8
Sinclair, John, 33
Singleton, John, 77
Sinon the Greek, 73
Sommersi, I, 32, 41, 42, 44, 47
Sonderkommandos, 34, 36, 37, 38, 43
SS, 12, 19, 37, 41, 75
Stangl, Franz, 53, 54, 59, *See* Treblinka
Sterba, James, 21
  The Demands of Justice, 21
Stewart, Honorable Potter, 24
Talio, 23, *See Lex Talionis*, *See also Contropasso*
Tartu, 74, *See* Linnas, Karl
Tchaikovsky, Peter Illich, 84
Third Reich, 11, 74
Tristi, I, 41, 42, 44-45, 47
Treblinka, 53, 74, *See* Stangl, Franz
Ugolino, Count, 1, 61, 70, 73

Ulysses, 1, 17, 24, 51, 62, 65, 67-69, 70
Useful/Useless Violence, 6, 12, 13
Vercors, Paul, 41
Villon, François, 79
   "La Ballade (des dames du temps jadis)," 79
Virgil, 33, 44, 46, 65, 69, 77

Volition (Intent), 10, 11, 17, 28, 45-46, 52, 54, *See Voluntas*
Voluntas, 72, 78, *See* Volition
Waldheim, Kurt, 40, 74-76, 83
Weisel, Eli, 15
Zurückschlagen, 25, *See* Améry, Jean